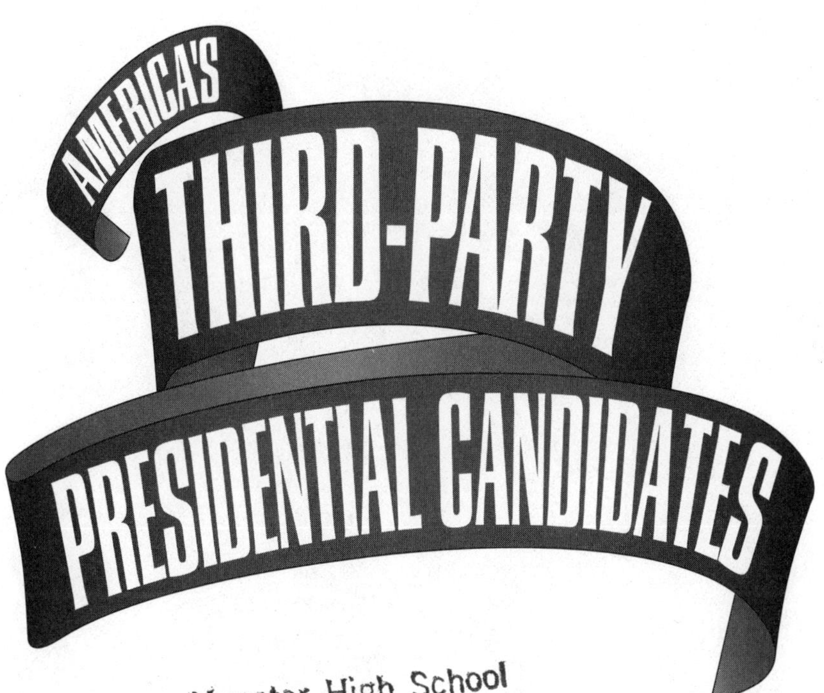
AMERICA'S
THIRD-PARTY
PRESIDENTIAL CANDIDATES

Nathan Aaseng

The Oliver Press, Inc.
Minneapolis

The Oliver Press, Inc.
Josiah King House
2709 Lyndale Avenue South
Minneapolis, MN 55408

Library of Congress Cataloging-in-Publication Data

Aaseng, Nathan.
America's third-party presidential candidates / Nathan Aaseng.
p. cm. — (Profiles)
Includes bibliographical references and index.
ISBN 1-881508-19-6
1. Presidential candidates—United States—Biography~~—Juvenile literature~~. 2. United States—Politics and government—20th century~~—Juvenile literature~~. 3. Presidents—United States—Election~~—Juvenile literature~~. I. Title. II. Series: Profiles (Minneapolis, Minn.)
~~E747.A28~~ 1995
324.973'09~~—dc20~~ 94-22102
~~CIP~~
~~AC~~

ISBN: 1-881508-19-6
Profiles XIV
Printed in the United States of America

99 98 97 96 95 8 7 6 5 4 3 2 1

Contents

Ross Perot, one of the most popular third-party candidates ever, speaks out during the first presidential debate of 1992.

Introduction

From the programs they can watch on television to the toppings they can put on their pizzas, the people of the United States expect to have a wide range of options. American voters, however, are not always pleased with the selection of candidates available during presidential elections. The traditional two-party system offers a choice between a Democrat and a Republican. Some Americans believe this is like choosing between vanilla and vanilla. Because both major parties try so hard to appeal to such a wide variety of voters, former Alabama governor George Wallace once declared, "there ain't a dime's worth of difference" between the two.

Even when Republican and Democratic candidates take opposing views, they frequently fail to impress the electorate. Voters often speak of "holding their nose" and casting their ballots for the "lesser of two evils." In 1980, more than half the eligible voters did not care for either Republican presidential candidate Ronald Reagan or Democratic incumbent Jimmy Carter. Public dissatisfaction with the two-party presidential choice ran nearly as high in 1992, when Democrat Bill Clinton challenged Republican incumbent George Bush.

Americans, however, have far more choices in presidential elections than many realize. Hundreds of political parties have sprung up over the course of U.S. history. More than 100 third-party candidates have attempted to win votes in presidential elections, and at least a dozen of these have claimed a spot on the official presidential ballot.

Although there are more than three political parties, the term *third party* is used to describe any political party other than Democratic or Republican. But because the U.S. political system is heavily stacked against third-party candidates, seldom does more than one of these smaller parties receive national attention during an election. Third-party candidates must first work through a jumble of state and federal filing requirements merely to get on the ballot. Although newspapers and television networks give Democratic and Republican presidential candidates thorough coverage during election years, third-party candidates are usually overlooked and must struggle to get their message out to the voters.

Unlike the two major party candidates, third-party candidates don't receive federal financial support unless they appear on the ballot in at least ten states and unless a candidate from their party has received at least five percent of the popular vote in a previous presidential election. Even with those funds, third parties usually must run low-budget campaigns while Democrats and Republicans spend millions of dollars.

Perhaps the most difficult barrier facing third-party candidates is simply that of habit. Americans have grown so accustomed to voting for either a Republican or a Democrat that they continue to do so even when they are not satisfied with these parties. Many voters who believe a third-party candidate is better qualified than the Democratic or Republican opponent are reluctant to "waste" their vote on someone who has virtually no chance to win.

The two-party format is so entrenched in people's minds that some people have even questioned the right of third parties to exist. In 1980, Republican national chairman Bill Brock angrily charged that John Anderson's third-party candidacy was "an assault on both parties and the political system." With the system rigged so firmly against them, most third-party candidates attract less than one percent of the vote. But occasionally a third-party nominee creates political waves big enough to frighten the major party candidates.

This book profiles eight third-party candidates, most of whom had to jump numerous political hurdles to win public support and make their platforms known. Only through their colorful personalities or sheer determination did these candidates acquire the attention and relative success that they did.

Before the two-candidate tradition became established in the United States, politicians staged an occasional battle between several candidates. In 1824, four candidates representing different groups within the Democratic-Republican Party faced off in the national election. Andrew Jackson won the popular vote, but he could not claim a majority of the electoral vote. The House of Representatives was forced to break the standoff and chose second-place finisher John Quincy Adams instead of Jackson. Twelve years later, the Whigs—who formed in opposition to the Democratic-Republicans—offered four candidates of their own.

The first of the third parties to make a significant impact on U.S. politics grew out of the anti-slavery movement in the northern states in the decades before the Civil War. The Liberty Party attracted only two percent of the votes in the 1844 presidential election, but its members combined with those who advocated cheap land in the slave-free territories in the Upper Midwest to form the Free Soil Party. Former Democratic president Martin Van Buren ran for president on the Free Soil ticket in 1848. He received about ten

John Quincy Adams (1767-1848) defeated Andrew Jackson and other members of the Democratic-Republican Party in the 1824 election to become the nation's sixth president in 1825.

Andrew Jackson (1767-1845) ran again for president in 1828—this time as a Democratic candidate—and defeated incumbent John Quincy Adams, then a National Republican. Jackson served as president from 1829 to 1837.

percent of the vote. This was enough to swing the election from Democrat Lewis Cass to Whig candidate Zachary Taylor. Members of the Whig and Free Soil parties then helped to form the Republican Party, which solidified into the Democrats' main opposition.

In 1856, both Republicans and Democrats faced a strong challenge from the American Party, which grew out of secret Protestant societies that feared and hated Roman Catholics. Party members were often called "Know-Nothings" because they would answer "I know nothing" to queries about their group. The American Party wanted tight controls over immigration, particularly of Irish Catholics. Its platform proclaimed that "Americans must rule America," meaning only people who were born in the United States should be allowed to hold public office.

Former president Millard Fillmore ran for president under the American Party banner in 1856. He captured nearly 900,000 votes—about 22 percent of the total cast—and won in the state of Maryland. The American Party quickly disintegrated, however, when its members disagreed over the slavery issue and others grew suspicious of its secret nature and extreme intolerance.

The 1860 campaign saw the nation deeply divided over the issue of slavery. Southern Democrats nominated John Breckinridge of Kentucky for president while Northern Democrats chose Stephen Douglas of Illinois. Senator John Bell of Tennessee ran as a candidate of the new Constitutional Union Party, which was formed in an effort to hold the country together against the efforts of extreme pro-slavery and anti-slavery forces. Each of the candidates won several electoral votes and split the vote enough to tilt the election in favor of Republican Abraham Lincoln, who took office despite winning fewer than 2 million of the more than 4.6 million votes cast.

During the 1860s and 1870s, the Greenback Party was formed by people who favored increasing the amount of paper money in circulation. Their presidential candidate, Iowa lawyer James Weaver, won slightly more than 300,000 votes in the 1880 presidential election. The Greenbacks then evolved into a broader-based party. This new People's Party—sometimes called the Populist Party—drew its support from those people frustrated with a government that appeared to favor big business at the expense of small businesses and rural areas.

The People's Party worked for national control of railroads and the telegraph. They also demanded a larger money supply, and an income tax structured so the rich would have to pay a greater share of taxes than the poor. Running as a Populist, Weaver collected more than 1 million votes in 1892, about eight percent of the total cast. He finished first in the states of Colorado, Idaho, Kansas, and North Dakota. Support for the Populists lessened, however, as the Democrats—led by presidential

An 1892 campaign poster for People's Party presidential candidate James Weaver and vice-presidential candidate James Field

candidate William Jennings Bryan—began to incorporate many of the Populists' ideas.

Given the overwhelming obstacles in their way, why do third-party candidates continue to run? After all, none of them has ever been elected president, and only one—1912 Progressive candidate Theodore Roosevelt—ever finished as high as second place in a presidential election.

In spite of the overwhelming odds against them, third-party candidates run for office because of a burning conviction that something is wrong with "politics as usual." And, despite their failure to enter the White House, third-party candidacies have not been in vain. Third parties often provide the spark for new ideas and policies that the more cautious major parties are unable or unwilling to introduce. The major parties listen carefully to how the public responds to these third-party innovations. If the major parties detect widespread public approval, they may adopt these ideas. Graduated income tax and the direct election of U.S. senators are two important policies that third-party candidates pushed onto the national agenda.

In addition, third-party candidates often publicize controversial viewpoints that the major parties prefer to ignore. In 1992, Ross Perot forced presidential candidates Bill Clinton and George Bush to take seriously the campaign issue of reducing the ballooning national deficit.

Third-party candidates also realize that, under the right circumstances, a small percentage of votes can give them a great deal of power. In a presidential election, each state receives a number of electoral votes based on the state's population. Except on rare occasions, the candidate who wins the most votes in a state gets all of that state's electoral votes, and a candidate must get a majority of the electoral votes to win election as president.

In a tight race, a third-party candidate who wins as few as three or four states might be able to deny victory to one of the two major parties. In such a case, the U.S. House of Representatives would choose the president. Fear of this scenario may cause major party candidates to try to win the support of people who are considering voting for third-parties.

By attracting votes from the Democrats and Republicans, third-party candidates have influenced the outcome of elections. Progressive candidate Theodore Roosevelt sealed William Howard Taft's defeat in 1912 by drawing away Republican votes that would have gone to Taft. During the 1948 election, Strom Thurmond cut into Harry Truman's majority by taking traditionally Democratic states away from him.

Even when third-party candidates fail to achieve any of their political goals, they provide an important outlet for expressing dissent. Strom Thurmond, Eugene V. Debs, and Henry A. Wallace campaigned on platforms that a vast majority of Americans rejected. Yet their candidacies provided a nonviolent means for a small but intense core of supporters to argue their case before the nation.

Above all other considerations, third-party candidates exist to provide alternatives to the nominees of the Democratic and Republican Parties. In 1980, independent candidate John Anderson said simply, "Our nation needs a choice in November. I want to offer that choice." Earlier, Progressive candidate Henry A. Wallace proclaimed, "I think the people are tired of having nothing but a choice between evils. They want a chance to vote for the greatest good, not the lesser evil."

The eight third-party candidates profiled in this book include liberals and conservatives, professional politicians and business leaders, northerners and southerners, publicity hounds and recluses, dreamy idealists and hard-nosed realists. All of these presidential candidates have fought against overwhelming odds to give Americans a greater range of choices in electing their president.

Theodore Roosevelt (1858-1919) left the Republican Party in 1912 to run for president as a "Bull Moose."

1

Theodore Roosevelt
The Bull Moose

Four years after leaving office, former Republican president Theodore Roosevelt fashioned the peculiar nickname for his new Progressive Party in one of his typically energetic outbursts. Arriving in Chicago for the 1912 Republican National Convention, where he hoped to take the nomination away from incumbent President William Howard Taft, Roosevelt declared he felt "like a bull moose." But when Taft received the Republican nomination, Roosevelt and his backers walked out and formed a third party.

Roosevelt, who had been president of the United States from 1901 to 1909, went on to prove his fitness in heroic fashion. Three weeks before the 1912 election, he brought his "Bull Moose" campaign to Milwaukee. As Roosevelt waved from an open car to a cheering throng of admirers, an assassin approached. John Schrank, a fanatic who resented Roosevelt for attempting to win a third term as president, walked within 30 feet of his target and fired a pistol at Roosevelt's chest.

The impact of the bullet spun Roosevelt around, but the shell struck his glasses case and the copy of the speech in his shirt pocket, then it slowed and deflected into the candidate's ribs. Roosevelt coughed to see if there was any blood in his lungs. Finding no blood, he

A smiling John Schrank (center) is taken into custody after attempting to assassinate Theodore Roosevelt. Schrank, a former saloonkeeper, would spend the rest of his life in a mental hospital.

deduced that the wound would not be fatal and went on campaigning.

Refusing medical treatment, Roosevelt entered a large auditorium filled with his backers and strode to the podium. He announced to the stunned crowd that he had just been shot and waved the speech pages with the bullet hole. "But it takes more than that to kill a Bull Moose," he thundered. Shouting in his usual high-pitched voice, Roosevelt delivered the 90-minute speech but agreed to go to a hospital when he was through. This incident vividly demonstrated the courage and flair that made Theodore Roosevelt the most successful third-party candidate in U.S. history.

Born on October 27, 1858, Theodore was the second child of a wealthy New York City family. While growing up, he was racked by severe asthma that often left him gasping for air. There was little evidence back then that young Theodore Roosevelt would grow into one of the most enduring politicians in U.S. history.

Because Theodore spent much of his childhood sick in bed, he was educated by private tutors instead of at school. He read books for hours on end, peering through thick glasses to compensate for his nearsightedness. His parents coddled him and spent a great deal of effort and money trying to cure his illnesses. Hoping that the clean air might offer some improvement, they sent him on trips to the country, sea shores, and the mountains.

As a teenager, Roosevelt gradually overcame his health problems. Self-conscious about his scrawny body from a childhood almost void of physical activity, he became determined to prove his "manhood," exercising in a gymnasium and taking boxing lessons. The future president often spoke of his admiration for courage and went out of his way to find dangerous situations to prove his own bravery. This attitude made Roosevelt extremely aggressive. He was absolutely convinced he was right about most subjects, especially on moral issues. Once he had made up his mind, no amount of discussion could dissuade him.

Theodore was studying at Harvard when his father died of cancer. The elder Roosevelt had believed the Christian duty of wealthy men was to give generously to charitable causes. He helped found a church, a hospital, a Children's Aid Society, and a YMCA in New York City.

Theodore was crushed by his father's death and dedicated himself to keeping alive his father's principles. Shortly after graduating from college and marrying Alice Hathaway Lee on his 22nd birthday, Roosevelt plunged into politics "to help the course of better government in New York." Like his father, he had inherited enough wealth to work toward social reforms without having to worry about making a living. Roosevelt became a Republican without hesitation. "A young man of my upbringing could join only the Republican Party," he explained.

In 1881, 23-year-old Roosevelt won election to the New York State Assembly and became its youngest member. Roosevelt wanted the government to create better working conditions in the squalid neighborhoods of New York City, where working people were struggling to survive. He had nothing but contempt for former president Thomas Jefferson's philosophy that the government should not become involved in the day-to-day lives of its citizens. The social conscience that his father had cultivated in Roosevelt would influence him throughout his entire political life.

As a newly elected assemblyman, Roosevelt realized he would have to battle hard against the firmly entrenched system of government. He had seen first-hand a display of political power when the U.S. Senate rejected his father's nomination for a federal post despite the elder Roosevelt's admirable qualifications.

The challenge of attacking the rich and the powerful appealed both to Roosevelt's sense of duty and his notion of courage. He pitched headlong into battle against what he called the "wealthy criminal class"—the rich business leaders, judges, lawyers, and politicians who controlled the government and lined their own pockets at public expense. When he attacked the practices of Jay Gould, one of the wealthiest and most powerful men in the nation, many people thought Roosevelt was committing political suicide. He further irritated Republicans by working with Grover Cleveland, the Democratic governor of New York, in trying to get rid of some of the most blatant abuses of government.

Roosevelt proclaimed he didn't care if he were run out of politics as long as he had "the feeling that I had done what was right." His enemies tried almost everything to stop him—from ridiculing his squeaky voice and toothy appearance, to blackmail and outright bribery—but Roosevelt refused to back down. His relentless fight for reform made him the most famous politician in New York state while he was still in his mid-twenties.

Roosevelt's wife, Alice, died of kidney disease on St. Valentine's Day in 1884, two days after giving birth to a baby girl. Roosevelt's mother had died of typhoid fever earlier on the same day. To overcome his deep sorrow, Roosevelt left politics for a time and worked on a cattle ranch in the Bad Lands of what is now North Dakota.

In 1886, Roosevelt married Edith Carow, a friend from childhood. He then accepted political appointments as commissioner of the U.S. Civil Service, president of the New York City Police Board, and assistant secretary of the U.S. Navy. Eager for more chances to test his courage and vigor, Roosevelt pressed strongly for war with Spain when that country attempted to end a rebellion in its colony of Cuba. After the Spanish-American War began in 1898, Roosevelt organized and led the volunteer regiment known as the "Rough Riders," and that unit earned national fame for their courageous fighting to capture Santiago, Cuba.

Theodore Roosevelt became a national hero in the United States after he served as captain of the "Rough Riders" during the Spanish-American War. The U.S. regiment won fame at the Battle of San Juan.

After the war, Roosevelt's political success grew rapidly. He won a term as New York's governor in 1898, then accepted the Republican nomination as vice-president in 1900. William McKinley, running for reelection on the Republican ticket, won the election but was killed in September 1901 by an assassin's bullet.

At the age of 42, Roosevelt became the youngest president in U.S. history. He quickly embarked on an energetic program of labor reforms, fiscal conservation, and regulation of powerful industries. He also drew

William McKinley (1843-1901), who was elected to his first term as president in 1896, was shot by an anarchist on September 5, 1901, and died nine days later. When Theodore Roosevelt replaced McKinley, Roosevelt's second wife, Edith (1861-1948), became First Lady of the United States.

praise for his firm foreign policy of preparing for conflicts, but not initiating hostilities. He summed up this philosophy in the words, "Speak softly and carry a big stick."

After serving most of McKinley's four-year term and easily winning reelection in 1904, Roosevelt bowed out of the presidency when his term came to an end. At that time, he used his influence to help win Republican Party support for the presidential candidacy of William Howard Taft, whom Roosevelt considered a capable administrator. Taft was elected president in November 1908 and took office the following year.

Taft, however, proved a bitter disappointment to Roosevelt. More conservative than Roosevelt, Taft frequently sided with the industrialists, wealthy landowners, and powerful political bosses whom Roosevelt had battled so diligently during his political career. Even when he agreed with Roosevelt, Taft did not possess the energy, flair, or persuasiveness to accomplish his goals. When the former president wrote to him expressing his concerns about the course of the nation, Taft admitted "my method has not worked out so smoothly."

In Roosevelt's eye Taft had become little more than a "yes man" for powerful special-interest groups. Because the president's ineptness was hurting both the nation and the Republican Party, Roosevelt and other Republicans grew disgusted with Taft. A group of people who called themselves the National Progressive Republicans organized at the home of Senator Robert M. La Follette of Wisconsin in January 1911. Dedicating themselves to giving ordinary people more voice in government, these politicians advocated the direct election of U.S. senators by the people, as well as party primaries to give the people a voice in choosing candidates for office and opportunities to express their wishes through petitions.

At this point, the progressive Republicans had not thought of forming a third party. But many party members wanted Roosevelt to challenge Taft for the Republican presidential nomination in 1912. Their request put Roosevelt in a difficult situation. Although

Roosevelt believed that Taft's decisions were hurting the Republican Party, he feared that challenging Taft would divide the party in half and hurt Republican chances of winning the next presidential election.

Roosevelt also knew that opposing Taft would be an outright admission that he had blundered in endorsing him four years earlier. Furthermore, Roosevelt had said in his victory speech on election night in 1904 that he would not seek the presidency again. Running again could make Roosevelt look like a liar. "I am not a candidate," he declared in 1911. "I will never be a candidate."

Senator Robert M. La Follette had no qualms about upsetting party unity. Convinced that Taft had to go, La Follette announced on June 17, 1911, that he would challenge him for the Republican Party nomination.

Roosevelt continued to give Taft the benefit of the doubt until the autumn of 1911. But when Taft fired Gifford Pinchot (a member of the National Forestry Commission and a friend of Roosevelt), then opposed Roosevelt's policy in a Justice Department suit against the U.S. Steel Corporation, Roosevelt's patience ran out. He complained that Taft had "completely twisted around the policies I advocated and acted upon."

Progressive Republicans, aware of Roosevelt's national popularity, believed the former president had a better chance than La Follette of defeating Taft. Seven Republican governors wrote to Roosevelt, urging him to seek the nomination, and "Roosevelt for President" clubs sprang up across the country.

Roosevelt's sense of responsibility finally combined with his large ego to nudge him back into presidential politics. As the person most responsible for getting Taft elected president, he reluctantly agreed it was his responsibility to remove Taft from office. Once Roosevelt decided on a course of action, he pursued it aggressively. "The fight is on, and I am stripped to the buff!" he announced in declaring his candidacy for the Republican nomination.

In 1912, Theodore Roosevelt hoped to win the presidency and return to the White House.

Roosevelt's entry into the race sank La Follette's effort. Although the Wisconsin senator continued to campaign, many of his early backers shifted to Roosevelt. Meanwhile, La Follette's remaining core of backers accused the former president of stabbing the Wisconsin senator in the back. Roosevelt had let La Follette take the risk of openly opposing Taft and had declared his intention to run only when he had seen that the coast was clear. Democrats and Taft supporters added their own criticism of Roosevelt, calling him a liar for breaking his promise not to run for the presidency again and accusing him of being a pompous, power-hungry egomaniac.

Never one to be swayed by criticism, Roosevelt declared that Taft had "brains less than a guinea pig" and launched an energetic campaign for the Republican nomination. At that time, only 12 states had primaries in which voters could express their preference for their party's candidate. Roosevelt won victories in nine state primaries, while La Follette captured two primaries, and Taft won only one.

Although the primary voters clearly wanted Roosevelt, Taft controlled the Republican leaders, who overwhelmingly sent Taft supporters as their representatives to the national convention in Chicago. At that convention, the rules committee ensured Taft's nomination by awarding 235 convention seats to Taft's delegates and only 19 seats to Roosevelt's.

With Taft securing the Republican nomination, Roosevelt could stay in the race only by running as a third-party candidate. From a practical standpoint, Roosevelt would have been better off admitting defeat and regrouping his forces for a run four years later in 1916. Even if Taft were reelected in 1912, he probably would not run again in 1916. With no sitting president in control of the party, Roosevelt would have had a clear path back to the presidency and a chance to undo the damage Taft had done.

Roosevelt, however, was not willing to let the blatant display of power politics by the Taft forces go unchallenged. In his mind, the voters had spoken clearly in the primaries. Yet, Taft's supporters at the convention had bulldozed the wishes of the electorate. The party, therefore, had broken faith with the people. As loyal as Roosevelt was to the Republican Party, he felt a greater loyalty to the people he believed the party had betrayed. Joining the furious Republicans who had walked out of the convention to form the Progressive Party—sometimes called Bull Moose Progressives—Roosevelt agreed to be this new party's candidate for president. Governor Hiram Johnson, California's popular crusader against political corruption, became their vice-presidential candidate.

The Progressive Party was passionately concerned about reforming the government to guarantee everyone a voice in the nation's affairs. The Progressives proposed

Hiram Johnson (1866-1945), Theodore Roosevelt's running mate in 1912, served three terms as governor of California and five terms as one of the state's U.S. senators.

an ambitious program of new policies. They called for several reforms, which would 1) give women the right to vote, 2) expose corruption in government, 3) regulate political lobbyists, 4) build new roads, 5) regulate business monopolies, 6) establish a graduated income tax and an inheritance tax, and 7) create a federal department of labor to abolish child labor, create unemployment insurance, and institute an eight-hour work day.

The Progressives considered themselves crusaders fighting a moral battle against a corrupt establishment. Roosevelt served as a powerful leader for this group. While he had slowed somewhat since his days as president, Roosevelt continually drew large and enthusiastic crowds.

The Democrats recognized that Roosevelt was more popular with voters than Taft. Having been shut out of the White House for 16 years, the Democratic Party devised a strategy that would neutralize Roosevelt's appeal while taking advantage of the Republican split. Therefore, they did not choose a conservative to draw votes away from Taft; they would let the president have those votes to himself. Instead, they selected a

During election years, political candidates—like 1912 Progressive candidate Theodore Roosevelt—use ribbons, buttons, bumper stickers, posters, lawn signs, and other items to promote their campaigns.

progressive Democrat named Woodrow Wilson to hold on to reform-minded Democrats who might otherwise vote for Roosevelt.

The strategy worked. Woodrow Wilson won the election with 6.3 million votes, about 42 percent of the total cast. Still, Roosevelt gained some personal satisfaction from beating Taft, 4.1 million votes to 3.5 million. Unlike many third-party candidates who appeal to a particular region or specific group of people, Roosevelt ran well in both urban and rural areas in most parts of the United States. He won the states of Pennsylvania, Michigan, Minnesota, South Dakota, and Washington, as well as 11 of California's 13 electoral votes. (Wilson received the other 2 electoral votes from California.) Roosevelt finished second in 23 other states. Altogether, he captured 27.4 percent of the popular vote—the highest percentage any third-party candidate has ever received in U.S. history.

When the election results were counted, Roosevelt summed up the campaign by saying, "We have fought the good fight, we have kept the good faith, and we have nothing to regret." Having helped rid the country of his controversial presidential successor, Roosevelt returned to the Republican Party, where he continued to advocate progressive policies until his death in 1919.

After leaving the White House, William Howard Taft (1857-1930) became chief justice of the Supreme Court in 1921—and was much happier in that position.

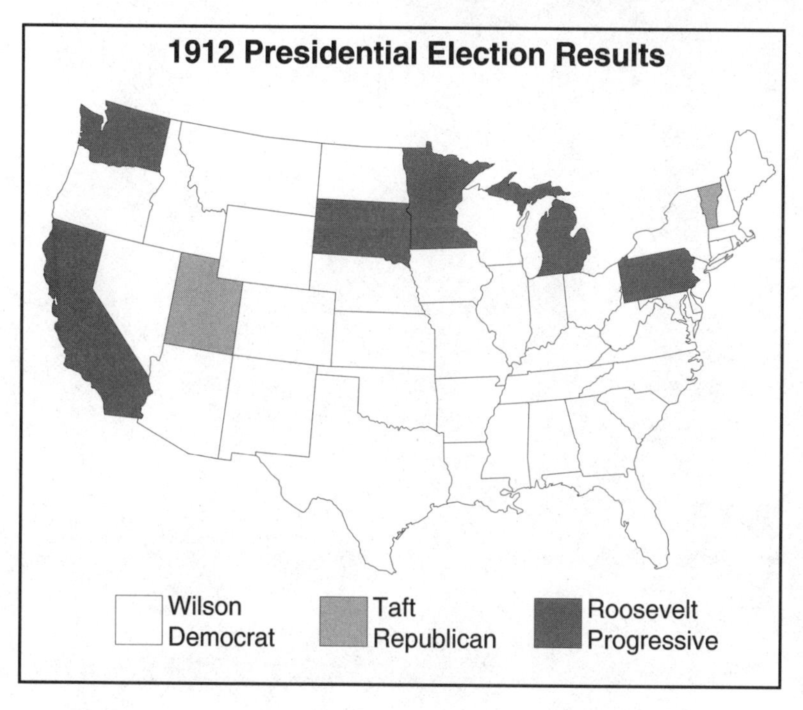

With 88 electoral votes, Theodore Roosevelt came in second place during the 1912 presidential election. He lost to Democratic candidate Woodrow Wilson's 435 electoral votes but far outnumbered Republican incumbent William Howard Taft's 8 electoral votes.

After losing his first presidential race in 1900, Socialist candidate Eugene V. Debs (1855-1926) ran for president again, and again, and again, and again.

2

Eugene V. Debs
The Gentle Radical

If personal character were the prime factor in presidential elections, Eugene V. Debs would have laid a strong claim on the White House. Even his fiercest detractors conceded that he was a man of integrity—a man who lived in poverty for years because he felt obliged to assume the debts of an organization he supported; a man who faced imprisonment rather than submit to a law that he felt robbed citizens of an important individual freedom.

Debs was an inspiring individual who dedicated himself to solving difficult problems and moving others into action. Yet, despite a dedicated core of supporters, Debs attracted a combined total of fewer than 3 million votes in his five runs for the presidency. Only once, in 1912, did he claim as much as 6 percent of the vote. In fact, a great number of Americans viewed him as a menace to society, and President Woodrow Wilson never changed his belief that Debs was a traitor to his country. Debs's problem was that he was a Socialist in a country where many people looked upon socialism as a national threat that needed to be stopped. In the long run, he fell short of persuading voters to believe in his cause.

Eugene Victor Debs was not a foreign agitator who tried to inflict his ideas on the United States. Born in Terre Haute, Indiana, on November 5, 1855, he was the

Though a liberal thinker about many political issues, Woodrow Wilson (1856-1924)—who served as president from 1913 to 1921—did not trust Socialist leader Eugene V. Debs.

third of Jean Daniel and Marguerite Debs's six children. Eugene was named after two writers whom his father admired, Eugene Sue and Victor Hugo, and Hugo's *Les Miserables* later became Eugene's favorite book.

Eugene's parents were immigrants from the province of Alsace-Lorraine, a stretch of land along the border between France and Germany that both countries claimed was theirs. The Debs family was a shining example of the "American Dream." They had arrived almost penniless in the United States in 1849. Through years of working at low-paying manual jobs, they established a modest but secure home for their family. Eventually, they saved enough to open their own grocery store and butcher shop.

Because of their parents' efforts, Eugene and his siblings were able to enjoy a middle-class life. Eugene especially enjoyed going on hunting and fishing trips with his father and younger brother, Theodore. After attending private school for several years, Eugene transferred into the Terre Haute public school system.

At age 14, Eugene dropped out of high school, which was not unusual for boys to do at that time, and took a job with the Terre Haute and Indianapolis Railway. Debs worked for five years as a locomotive cleaner and a firefighter, while his mother fretted about such hazards as engines blowing up. Eugene V. Debs finally quit working for the railway in 1874 and got a job as a billing clerk.

In his mid-twenties, Debs became involved in local politics and was elected city clerk of Terre Haute. After serving two terms as city clerk, he sought a greater challenge and was elected to the Indiana state legislature in 1885. That year, Eugene married Katherine Metzel, the daughter of a drug store owner. Debs was so forthright and honest as a politician that, after assessing his performance as a lawmaker, he decided he had not been effective enough to deserve reelection and declined to run for another term.

Debs always felt a special attachment to working-class people, an attitude he shared with his father, Jean Daniel Debs, who had been brought up in a wealthy, highly educated family in Europe. But when Jean Daniel fell in love with Marguerite, a common millworker, his father forbade them from getting married. Jean Daniel Debs had to choose between his love and the family fortune that he would inherit by obeying his father's wishes. Rejecting the wealth, he married Marguerite and sailed to the United States to start a new life.

Eugene continued his active involvement with working people through the Brotherhood of Locomotive Firemen (BLF) union years after he had quit working for the railroad. At that time, most labor unions were loosely organized, often short-lived collections of workers with little influence in contract negotiations or politics. The BLF was concerned primarily with banding together to provide insurance for its members and to make contributions to charitable causes. It suffered from weak leadership and a shortage of money.

When the union members asked Debs to serve as secretary-treasurer, they relocated the BLF to Terre Haute. Almost single-handedly, Debs kept the union in operation. When it ran out of funds, he contributed his own money. When that did not prove enough to keep the union going, he went into debt and took out personal loans backed by his family's credit.

Debs arrived on the union scene at a crucial time in U.S. labor relations. Mass production methods had allowed many factory owners to grow rich while their employees lived in poverty. The injustices grew so outrageous that many citizens began to question the traditional American belief that owners had the right to operate their businesses however they wished. But all the money and political influence was on the side of the employers. Looking for a way to fight for the right to a decent life, workers turned to unions to provide them with strength in numbers.

The leaders of the Brotherhood of Locomotive Firemen were reluctant to bring the demands of their members—especially a right-to-strike provision—to management. In 1885, the BLF members grew frustrated with the lack of improvement in their working conditions and voted most of their officers out, except for Debs. Since he also opposed the idea of strikes, Debs decided to resign as well. But the union's members were so impressed by his dedication that they persuaded him to remain in office. Debs spent the remaining years of the decade trying to get the members of the other railroad unions to join together so they would all have more clout in dealing with management. In 1889, he appeared to have organized several small unions into a federation. But the federation collapsed within three years. Debs continued to edit a journal for railroad workers, but he backed off from leadership roles in the union movement for a few years.

When an economic depression in 1893 hit workers hard with pay cuts and layoffs, Debs redoubled his efforts to organize rail workers. This time, his American Railway Union (ARU) won some surprising concessions from James J. Hill's Great Northern Railroad. This success convinced many unskilled workers that the union provided a real hope for decent wages and working conditions. By its second year, ARU membership had swelled to more than 150,000, making it one of the largest unions in the nation.

The following year, the Pullman Sleeping Car Company of Chicago cut wages while raising the price of the goods the company sold to its employees. Since many employees depended on the company store and company housing, this policy imposed a great hardship on them. In May 1894, the angry workers went on strike, and American Railway members backed them by refusing to work on any train that carried Pullman cars.

Chicago newspapers labeled the action "Debs' Rebellion." Ironically, Debs had argued against the strike.

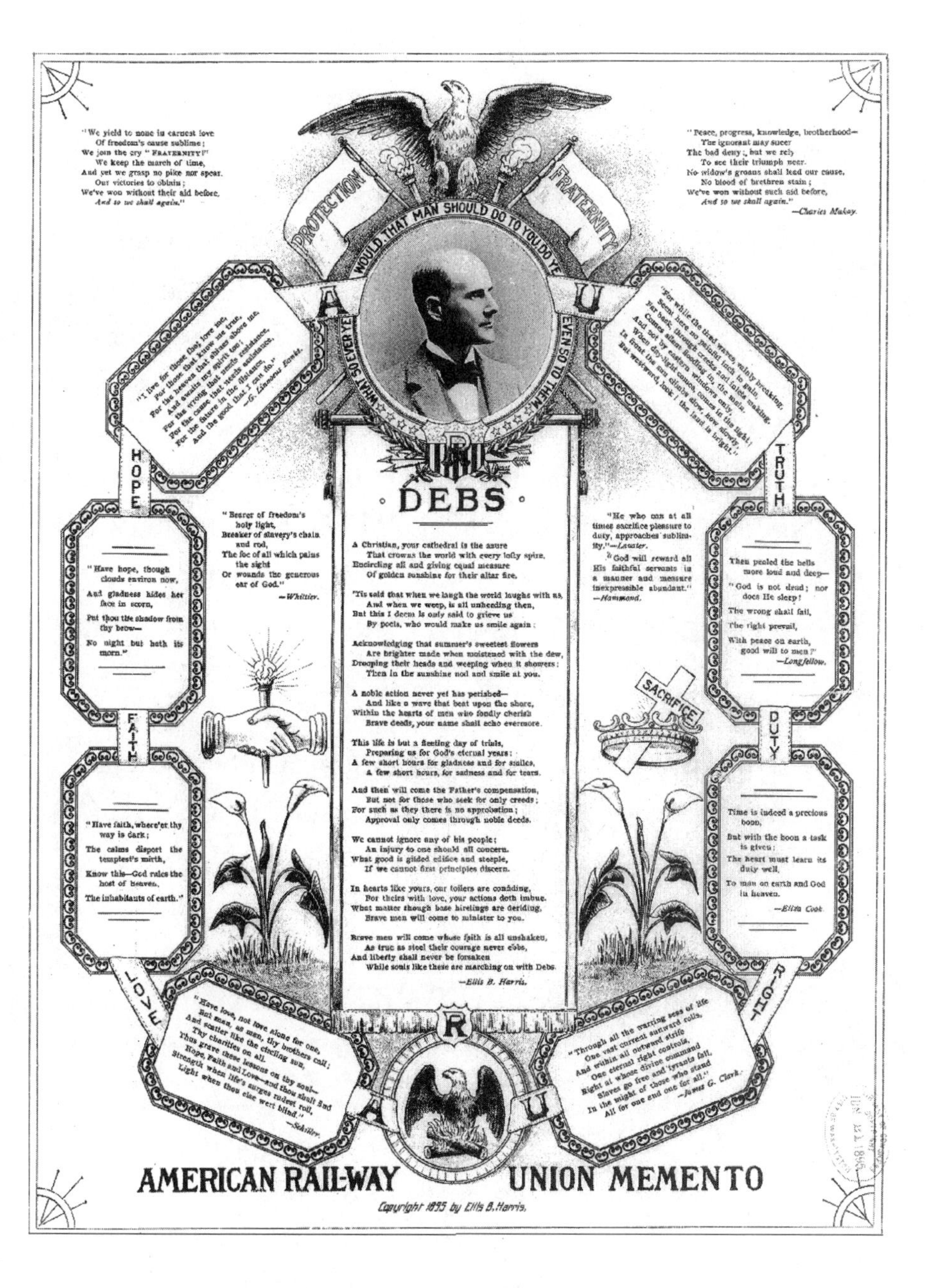

This 1895 poster expressed Eugene V. Debs's values for the American Railway Union.

Doubting that Pullman would back down, he feared a prolonged or failed strike would hurt the union movement. Debs, however, was committed to majority rule. Once the union members voted to strike, he did his best to carry out their wishes. Debs urged the strikers to avoid violence, but when President Grover Cleveland ordered in federal troops to disperse the strikers, the tense situation quickly flared out of control. The resulting riots killed 30 people and wounded 60 more.

A federal court then stepped in on the side of the Pullman Company, ordering the ARU officers to stop all activities concerning the strike. The U.S. Supreme Court supported this ruling with an opinion that the government had the right to stop a strike in the interest of the public welfare.

Refusing to abandon his union members, Debs ignored the court order. That action landed him in prison for six months on a charge of civil contempt. With Debs locked up, the strike and the ARU lost support. When he returned from prison, Debs found that the union had left behind a mountain of debt. For the next 18 years, Debs worked to pay off the debt—primarily with his earnings from lectures.

The burden of debt also weighed heavily on his wife. Eugene and Katherine Debs had no children, and Eugene was so involved in his causes that he was seldom home. In an effort to make his wife happy, Debs had built a large house in a wealthy neighborhood.

Although Katherine Debs worked briefly as her husband's secretary, she seldom became directly involved with his business and political endeavors during their 41 years of marriage.

Meanwhile, Debs's time in prison had steered him in a new direction. While incarcerated, he had read extensively about socialism and had become convinced that the U.S. system of private ownership would never allow workers to escape their poverty. He saw the practice of socialism, which supported government control of many businesses and spreading society's wealth more equally among the people, as the solution to the workers' plight.

When Debs was released from prison, he helped to form the Social Democratic Party of America. In 1900, the new party changed its name to the Socialist Party of America. Many workers admired Debs's courage in going to prison rather than abandoning his union, and they joined his movement by the thousands. His earnest and persuasive public speaking ability won him additional supporters.

The Socialist Party of America called for public ownership of utilities and public transportation. Party members insisted on better working conditions and on a living wage for all workers. They also advocated public work projects to reduce unemployment, national insurance for all people, and equal rights for women.

Unfortunately, Debs was no more comfortable with politics in the early twentieth century than he had been in his days as a failed state legislator in the late nineteenth century. He liked to build a consensus on issues, with everyone working together. Infighting among small factions within the party bewildered him. In fact, some of the more practical, hard-nosed Socialists found his self-righteous nature and sentimental idealism hard to swallow. Despite being the clear champion of the Socialist Party, Debs was so discouraged by the constant bickering that he avoided most Socialist conventions.

Nonetheless, the Socialists believed in Debs and repeatedly nominated him for president. When he first ran for president in 1900 against Republican William McKinley, Debs drew fewer than 100,000 votes. Although his Socialist Party began to gather support, some opposing politicians blasted Debs as a dangerous and muddled thinker.

In the next few years, Debs made few inroads into the public's strong support for Theodore Roosevelt—who had become president after McKinley's assassination in 1901—and Roosevelt's successor, William Howard Taft. In 1904, Debs attracted just over 400,000 votes—roughly 3 percent of the total.

Running a dramatic campaign in 1908 from a train known as the "Red Special," Debs increased his total votes to only 420,000. As Taft began to turn away from Roosevelt's progressive policies, though, public discontent soared, and Progressive reformer Robert M. La Follette

A 1904 campaign poster for Eugene V. Debs and his vice-presidential candidate, Ben Hanford

During the 1908 presidential campaign, Eugene V. Debs rode across the country in his "Red Special" locomotive.

kicked off a wild presidential campaign by challenging Taft for the 1912 Republican nomination.

The final ballot that year listed four well-known candidates: Taft for the Republicans, Roosevelt for the Progressives, Woodrow Wilson for the Democrats, and Debs for the Socialists. Even though Debs came in fourth place, far behind the triumphant Wilson, the Socialist candidate more than doubled his previous vote. The final tally showed Debs with about 900,000 votes—approximately 6 percent of the total votes cast.

Although the Socialist Party was growing, Debs declined to run for president in 1916. However, he continued editing the Socialist weekly newspaper, *Appeal to Reason*. In his editorials, Debs denounced capitalism as the main cause of evil in society. He also criticized the Wilson administration for bringing the United States to the brink of war in Europe. He saw World War I as a fight to protect the interests of the wealthy. When the United States entered the war in 1917, the Socialist Party protested loudly. Many Americans said the Socialists were traitors for not supporting the war effort. The U.S. Congress, in fact, passed legislation outlawing any speech that opposed American war policies.

Debs argued that these laws were contrary to the freedoms guaranteed by the U.S. Constitution. He traveled throughout the Midwest, speaking out against the war and daring authorities to arrest him. On June 18, 1918, a few weeks after Debs had delivered a speech in Canton, Ohio, they finally did. The government prosecuted him under the Espionage Act of 1917. A federal court convicted Debs and sentenced him to ten years in prison. The U.S. Supreme Court denied his appeal, and President Wilson refused to issue Debs a pardon.

Undaunted, the Socialists nominated Debs for president again in 1920. Their platform declared, "The outgoing administration, like Democratic and Republican administrations of the past, leaves behind it a disgraceful record of solemn pledges unscrupulously broken and public confidence ruthlessly betrayed." Despite being confined in an Atlanta, Georgia, prison, Debs received approximately 920,000 votes—the highest number of his career.

While in prison, Debs slipped into poor health. Fearing that Debs's death while behind bars would energize the Socialists and attract sympathy to their cause, President Warren G. Harding ordered the Atlanta prison to release Debs on Christmas Day 1921.

Eugene V. Debs and some visiting supporters hear the results of the 1920 election from his prison cell.

Five runs for the presidency against hopeless odds were enough for Debs. In 1924, he threw his support to Robert M. La Follette's third-party bid. Two years later, the Socialist Party of America lost its driving force when Eugene V. Debs died of a heart attack at the age of 70.

Following Debs's death, New Yorker Norman Thomas became the new leader of the Socialist Party. In the tradition of Eugene V. Debs, Thomas ran for president repeatedly, campaigning in 1928, 1932, 1936, 1940, 1944, and 1948. He achieved his strongest support during the 1932 election, when he received nearly 885,000 votes. But Thomas—like Debs—failed to win even one electoral vote during any of his bids for the presidency. By 1955, when Thomas resigned as leader of the party, socialism had faded into the background of the American political scene.

Although the Socialist Party did not thrive in Debs's absence, his lifelong effort had not been completely in vain. Several causes that he advocated, such as increased government protection of workers and greater rights for women, have taken root in American society.

Robert M. La Follette (1855-1925), a respected senator and political reformer, believed that major political changes were impossible under the two-party system.

3

Robert M. La Follette
Fighting Bob

While many third-party candidates have had to struggle to get the media and the voters to pay attention to them, Robert M. La Follette had no such problem. When he decided to champion a cause, he charged onto center stage, bristling with the fury of a righteous avenger. Showing the dramatic skills that earned him a reputation as one of the best trial lawyers in Wisconsin, the senator usually held his audience spellbound.

"Now his face was calm—now a thundercloud—now full of sorrow," reported the *Wisconsin State Journal* in 1900 about La Follette's courtroom oratory. "Here his voice arose almost to a shriek—there it sank to a whisper."

La Follette's dramatics were masterful, and his outrage was genuine. Early in his career, the arrogance of party bosses who ignored the wishes of the voters incensed this Wisconsin politician. He fumed over losing nominations for office to individuals who used wealth and political connections to manipulate the election. Above all, he was shocked by the growing gulf in society between the wealthy few and the masses of poor people.

Agreeing with both Progressive Party leader Theodore Roosevelt and Socialist Eugene V. Debs, La Follette believed that the United States needed to use the power of government to work for the common good. His methods for achieving that aim, however, took a middle course between the two politicians. La Follette led a political movement known as Insurgency. An insurgent person rebels against authority—in this case, the leadership of the Republican Party. While the Insurgents did not advocate Socialism as Debs did, they demanded more sweeping changes than the Progressive supporters of Roosevelt. Roosevelt, in fact, defined Insurgents as "Progressives who were exceeding the speed limit."

"Fighting Bob" La Follette—as he was sometimes called—was so determined to rescue democracy from what he saw as the corrupt control of special-interest groups that he literally worked himself into exhaustion.

Robert Marion La Follette, the youngest of four children of a prosperous farm family, was born on June 14, 1855, in Primrose Township, Wisconsin. Robert was only eight months old when his father died. His mother, Mary, kept the farm but turned over its operations to a son-in-law. In 1862, when Robert was seven, she married a 70-year-old merchant named John Saxton. Mary moved her family to Saxton's home, about 20 miles from the Primrose farm. Believing that education was the key to a successful life, she gradually sold off sections of the farm to pay for Robert's education at good private schools.

When his stepfather's health began to fail, 15-year-old Robert moved the family back to Primrose and took charge of the farm. Always outgoing, young La Follette learned Norwegian so he could speak with his many Norwegian farm neighbors. He listened to their concerns so open-mindedly that he changed his political loyalty from his mother's Democratic Party to the Republican Party that his neighbors preferred.

Times were difficult for farmers in the 1870s, so Robert decided to continue his education to prepare for a different career. In 1875, his mother sold 80 more acres of farm land and moved to the city of Madison with Robert. There, his mother took in boarders so he could attend the University of Wisconsin at Madison. But even that was not enough to meet the family's needs, so Robert sold books and taught school while attending college.

During his years in college, La Follette became active in public speaking and politics. La Follette was selected as top orator in a competition among 10,000 Midwestern college students. During his final three years of college, La Follette edited the student newspaper. His editorials preached that people could advance as far as they wanted simply by working hard and living right. Oddly, he did not take his own advice; he became so involved in partying and politics that he failed to pay proper attention to his studies. As a result, La Follette almost didn't graduate and nearly wasted the great family sacrifice that had gone into his education.

During his junior year, La Follette became engaged to a student named Belle Case. (In 1885, this young woman from Baraboo, Wisconsin, became the first woman to graduate from the University of Wisconsin law school.) During their engagement, Belle taught school in Baraboo while Robert went on to law school. He passed the bar exam in 1880.

After graduating from law school, La Follette immediately jumped into the political life that he would come to enjoy. The 25-year-old lawyer was elected Dane County's district attorney. Still echoing the conservative Republican line, he won praise for his no-nonsense prosecution of tramps, drunks, and other "public nuisances." He and Belle married during his first term as district attorney.

Belle Case La Follette (1859-1931) earned a law degree in 1885, worked for the women's suffrage movement, and advised her husband, Robert, throughout his political career.

After four years as district attorney, La Follette set his sights on a higher political office. Aided by his spellbinding style of public speaking and the efforts of his campaign manager, Civil War general George Bryant, he easily won election to the U.S. House of Representatives in 1885. At age 30, La Follette was the youngest member of Congress at the time. Despite his relative youth, La Follette carried himself with such energy and confidence that he became the leader of Wisconsin's congressional delegation.

During this time, La Follette continued to look to prominent business leaders as role models. Their success proved to him the reality of the "American dream": that all people could advance as far as their efforts would carry them. He saw, however, one glaring exception to that principle—in the nation's treatment of blacks. This led him to speak strongly against racial discrimination as contrary to American ideals.

During his three terms as a Wisconsin representative, La Follette worked so hard for his district that one newspaper called him "the steadfast friend of every interest in his district." Still, his efforts were not enough to allow him to retain his seat in Congress. In the election of 1890, Wisconsin voters reacted angrily to unpopular state laws passed by Wisconsin Republicans. Although La Follette was not involved in the decisions of the state government, the voters' anger at the Republican Party swept him out of national office.

Following his defeat, La Follette returned to Madison to practice law. As he tried cases and traveled around the state, his admiration for businesses began to sour. He saw the wealthy using the law to dodge taxes while the poor were struggling with their increased tax burden. He also saw industrialists getting fabulously rich but giving almost nothing back to employees or to the community.

The economic depression of 1893 jolted La Follette's confidence in both the U.S. government and the American free-enterprise system. If the current system was so wonderful, he asked, why were 20 percent of the banks failing? Why were the streets filled with desperate, willing workers unable to find jobs? Worst of all, why were the wealthy splurging on luxuries when so many other Americans were suffering?

While La Follette agonized over these questions, he got a bitter taste of defeat. In 1894, he supported

Nils Haugen for the Republican nomination for governor of Wisconsin. After the incumbent beat Haugen, La Follette decided to run for governor in 1896 and take his campaign to the people. He organized his own network of friends and workers and spoke directly to voters. He came so close to winning in 1896 that he tried the same strategy again two years later.

By the time of the 1898 state convention in Milwaukee, La Follette had enough supporters among the delegates to win the Republican nomination for governor. But the powerful interest groups were not about to give up their control of the party. They quietly handed out money and promises to entice La Follette's delegates to change their votes. When the voting took place, his margin of victory had mysteriously disappeared, and he had again failed to gain the nomination.

This tactic convinced La Follette that arrogant party leaders were endangering American democracy. He argued that the United States needed to "go back to the first principles of democracy; go back to the people." He stepped up his campaign to "rid the Republican Party of corporation control and again make it the party it was in the days of Lincoln."

La Follette finally amassed enough popular support to overcome even the wealthiest and most powerful of his rivals. In 1900, he was elected governor of Wisconsin with 60 percent of the vote. Determined that the voters should never again be denied the candidates of their choice, he pushed through a law that called for direct primaries to choose party candidates for state office.

In 1906, La Follette carried his campaign for democracy to the nation by becoming one of Wisconsin's two U.S. senators. He immediately began taking on the power structure in Washington, D.C. By refusing to go along with the tradition that discouraged first-year senators from giving speeches on the Senate floor, "Fighting Bob" La Follette offended many veteran politicians. He shocked and frightened many others by making use of the role-call vote. Prior to La Follette, Congress often announced only the totals in controversial votes and did not say how individuals had voted. La Follette did his best to make sure the voters knew how their elected officials were voting on various issues.

With President Theodore Roosevelt working from the White House and La Follette in Congress, the federal government initiated many reforms to put the power of government to work for ordinary people instead of just for the wealthy. But when William Howard Taft took over as president in 1909, he often allied himself with the powerful special-interest groups that Roosevelt and La Follette had been fighting.

Taft's attitude dismayed many Republicans. Seeking an alternative to the president, they turned to La Follette to rescue the party. "Fighting Bob" took up the challenge with a vengeance. He hammered at industrial capitalists who made fortunes at the expense of their neighbors, and he criticized the party bosses who clung to power at the expense of democracy.

La Follette struck a nerve with the American people. On January 22, 1912, his appearance at Carnegie Hall in New York City nearly caused a riot among his enthusiastic supporters. Police had to call in reserves from two stations to control the thousands of people trying to cram into the building to hear La Follette speak.

The success La Follette was experiencing provided encouragement to former president Roosevelt, who had been mulling the possibility of getting back into politics and challenging Taft. Roosevelt's entrance into the race doomed La Follette's effort because Roosevelt was immensely popular. However, the Wisconsin senator continued to score some spectacular successes.

In 1912, La Follette won the North Dakota presidential primary with 58 percent of the vote, compared to 39 for Roosevelt and a dismal 3 percent for Taft. He swamped Taft by a three-to-one margin in Wisconsin's primary. But neither Roosevelt nor La Follette was able to overcome Taft's advantage among party regulars. Thus, Taft won the nomination at the Republican convention.

With help from discontented Republicans, Roosevelt went on to form the Progressive Party. But La Follette, bitter about Roosevelt's interference in the primaries, refused to support him. Instead, he stayed on the sidelines as Democratic candidate Woodrow Wilson won the election.

During Wilson's presidency, La Follette fought against the involvement of the United States in World War I, which had entangled most of Europe's major powers since 1914. La Follette saw the war as something favored by industrialists who stood to make money from the conflict by manufacturing military supplies for the government. In his attempt to keep the United States out of the war, La Follette asked for a national advisory referendum in 1916. The referendum would require the government to consult the public before declaring war. "The poor, sir, who are the ones called upon to rot in the trenches, have no organized power, but oh, Mr. President, at some time they will be heard," he declared. Nonetheless, on April 4, 1917, the U.S. Senate voted 82 to 6 to enter the war.

Throughout World War I, La Follette continued to champion the rights of ordinary Americans. Now the leader of the group of Progressives known as the Insurgency, he especially railed against laws such as the Espionage Act, which put Americans in jail for daring to question the country's involvement in the war in Europe. La Follette's stance attracted national scorn, and political leaders called him a traitor. In a speech given at the end of the war in 1918, he publicly said, "I would not change my record in the war for that of any man living or dead."

La Follette then pressed forward with his plans for cleaning up and rebuilding the U.S. system of government. He supported taxes as the best way to make sure the country's wealth was more evenly distributed among its citizens. He supported labor and agriculture and launched investigations into government corruption. His work in support of progressive programs was so effective that, despite the venom of his critics, he won reelection to the Senate in 1922 with 83 percent of the Wisconsin vote.

As the 1924 presidential campaign approached, Progressives began to despair over their choices. Republican President Calvin Coolidge was a conservative in the mold of Taft. Yet, the disorganized Democrats had little hope of defeating Coolidge. Progressives looked to their aging champion, "Fighting Bob" La Follette, for an alternative.

Vice-president Calvin Coolidge (1872-1933) became president of the United States in 1923, when President Warren G. Harding died in office.

As support swelled for a third-party challenge to Coolidge, La Follette's family begged him not to run. Sixty-eight years old and in poor health following a bout with pneumonia, La Follette was in no condition to launch a major campaign. Still, he was the only person with the clout and respect to present a serious challenge to the major candidates. Encouraged by a diverse following of farmers, laborers, church groups, Socialists, young idealists, intellectuals, and women (who had won the right to vote in 1920), La Follette charged into the campaign on July 3, 1924, as the head of the new Progressive Party, which was officially called the Conference for Progressive Public Action.

La Follette posed a simple question to voters: Were public officials serving the common good or exploiting it for their own gain? La Follette's party's platform condemned monopolies and called for nationalization of the railroads, collective bargaining for workers, economic protection for farmers, public works to combat unemployment, and the direct election of U.S. presidents.

La Follette tried to recruit U.S. Supreme Court justice Louis Brandeis to run as his vice-president. When Brandeis turned him down, La Follette turned instead to Burton Wheeler, a Montana senator who admired La Follette so much that he once ranked him with former presidents Thomas Jefferson and Abraham Lincoln as one the three greatest Americans. La Follette exerted a similar effect on his other supporters as he energized

Unlike Progressive presidential candidate Robert M. La Follette, who had been a Republican, vice-presidential candidate Burton Wheeler (1882-1975) had been a Democrat before joining the Progressive Party.

them with his firm convictions and dramatic speeches. In fact, he often attracted larger audiences than the major party candidates. At a stop in Cleveland, Ohio, he preached his message to a shouting sea of more than 20,000 admirers.

The campaign began as a contest between Republican incumbent Coolidge and La Follette. The Republicans fired away at the fighter from Wisconsin. Repeatedly charging that La Follette's untested policies would harm businesses and drive the nation into a depression, they warned that the choice was between "Coolidge or Chaos." The slogan touched a nerve. Many workers abandoned La Follette out of fear for their jobs, and even people who admired him were uneasy with some of his programs. Further doubts about La Follette bogged down the campaign. His opposition to World War I and

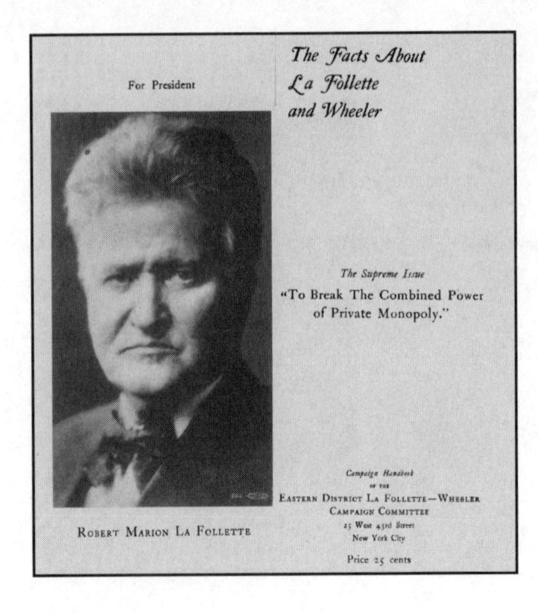

"The Facts About La Follette and Wheeler," a pamphlet summarizing their 1924 platform, sold for 25 cents.

his support of the Socialist movement disturbed many of his rural backers.

Another problem that La Follette faced was lack of campaign funds. As a third-party candidate and a champion of the common people, he had no access to major contributions. During the 1924 campaign, the Republicans outspent La Follette by a margin of 19 to 1, $4.2 million compared to $220,000.

Despite all of those obstacles, La Follette put up a respectable fight. The Progressive candidate captured 16.5 percent of the vote—nearly 5 million votes—compared to 54 percent for Coolidge and 29 percent for Democratic candidate John B. Davis. La Follette easily won his home state of Wisconsin and ran well throughout the West, finishing second in 11 states and narrowly missing victory in North Dakota and Minnesota.

La Follette could not have governed long had he been elected. His heart steadily deteriorated after the exhausting campaign until it gave out on June 18, 1925, four days after his 70th birthday. But his legacy has lasted longer than that of most third-party candidates. La Follette remains among the most revered politicians in the history of Wisconsin. In the years after his death, many of La Follette's proposals—including direct primaries, direct election of senators, and government-sponsored social programs—have come into existence.

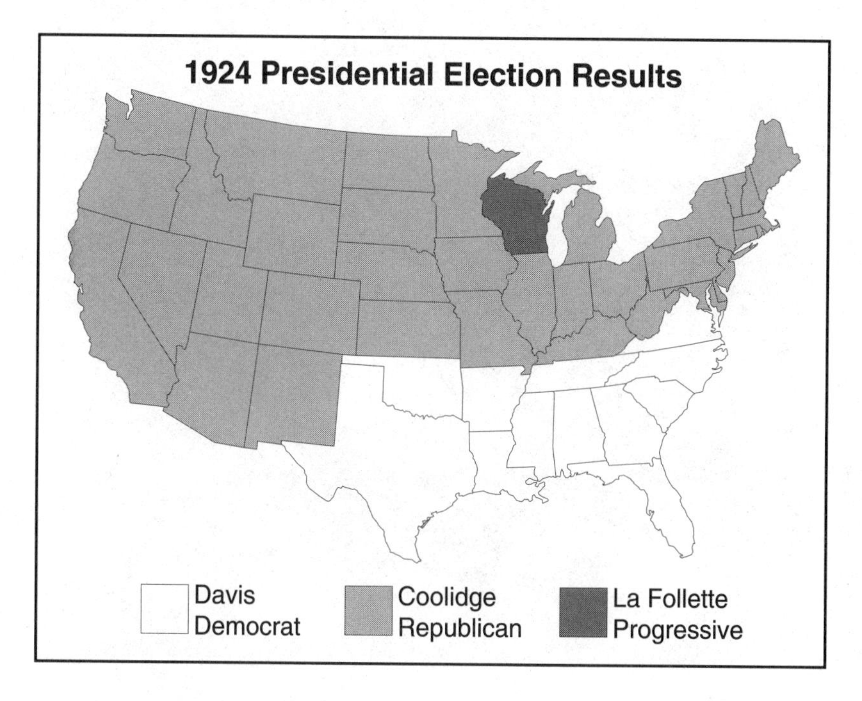

Republican Calvin Coolidge won the 1924 presidential election with 382 electoral votes, far exceeding Democrat John B. Davis's 136 votes, and Progressive Party candidate Robert M. La Follette's 13.

After serving as a Democratic vice-president, Henry A. Wallace (1888-1965) decided to try winning the presidency in 1948 as a third-party candidate.

4

Henry A. Wallace
The Philosopher Farmer

Had Henry A. Wallace test-marketed his appeal as a presidential candidate in 1948, he would have failed on virtually every count. Despite his position as a former vice-president, his impressive record as U.S. secretary of agriculture, and a reputation as a man of ideas, Wallace was a political disaster waiting to happen. In direct contrast to Robert M. La Follette, who led the Progressive Party during the 1920s, Wallace was a shy man and a mediocre public speaker. Caring little for image, he often appeared in public with uncombed hair and disheveled clothes.

Although Wallace was not the shrewdest or most personable politician, he lived by his own ideals and suggested new solutions to the problems of his times. But these solutions often angered the public. When asked in a 1951 interview what would have happened if he had been renominated as vice-president in 1944 and had risen to the presidency after President Franklin Roosevelt's death, Henry A. Wallace candidly admitted, "Anyone with my views would have run into the most extraordinary difficulties."

Instead of presenting a clear alternative to the Democratic and Republican parties, Wallace bewildered the electorate. In 1948, the *New York Times* called him the "most complex personality in American public life today." He was still registered as a Republican in 1932, when he gave $25 to the Socialists, yet voted for and helped to swing Iowa to the Democrats.

Henry A. Wallace knew he had little chance of winning the 1948 presidential election. Even though his family and friends urged him to stay out of a presidential campaign that could only tarnish his reputation, he felt compelled to "bear witness" to the cause of international peace. To some people, this puzzling man was a brilliant political innovator with the ability to help the nation. To others, he was a dangerous radical who would destroy the United States if elected president.

The name "Henry Wallace" had been well-known in the Midwest long before the 1948 third-party candidate had been born. His grandfather, "Uncle Henry" Wallace, had come to Iowa from Pennsylvania full of ideas about farming. His views on agriculture, which he published in a weekly newspaper called *Wallace's Farmer*, gained admiration throughout rural America. "Good farming is simply obedience to natural law, just as good living is obedience to moral law," he once wrote. "Uncle" Henry's son, Henry Cantwell Wallace, followed in his father's footsteps as a farmer-philosopher who helped to make *Wallace's Farmer* one of the most influential periodicals of its time. His son, presidential candidate Henry Agard Wallace, was born on his grandfather's farm in Adair County, Iowa, on October 7, 1888.

The third generation Henry Wallace spent much of his childhood in Ames, Iowa, where his father taught at the state agricultural college (now Iowa State University). The family had little money but held an intense interest in culture and education. The Wallace house was filled with books and the sounds of classical music. At the age of 6, Henry became friends with George Washington Carver, a 27-year-old student who would later become famous for his work with plants. Henry often tagged along with Carver and learned much about the science of growing plants.

With the earnings from *Wallace's Farmer*, young Henry's father bought a ten-acre farm. Henry enjoyed

Agricultural chemist George Washington Carver (1864?-1943) strengthened the southern economy by teaching farmers to improve their soil and diversify their crops.

gardening, working small plots of land to test new varieties of grain seed, and raising cows, hogs, and chickens. The shy boy was so uninterested in social niceties that he often went to school in clothes that reeked from his farm work.

After graduating from high school, Wallace attended the agricultural college at Ames. A serious, dedicated student, he had little time to make friends at school. Still, he managed to fall in love with Ilo Browne, and the two married in 1914, a year after Henry had earned his degree. Both of them enjoyed life on their farm six miles outside of Des Moines, Iowa. As part of his farm duties, Wallace woke at 4:30 A.M. every day to deliver milk to his customers in Des Moines.

Although farming required long hours of work, Wallace saved time to do what he loved best: experiment with new agricultural methods. He often stopped at the Des Moines public library and returned home with stacks of books on livestock production. He set aside test plots for evaluating his own experiments in plant breeding. In 1926, these experiments paid off when he founded the Hi-Bred Corn Company (later called the Pioneer Hi-Bred Corn Company).

Wallace's company produced the world's first high-yielding hybrid seed corn for commercial use. Wallace had such confidence in his product that he offered a special deal to farmers hard-pressed by tough economic times: If they would plant half their crop with ordinary seed and half with his hybrid and then pay him a portion of the increased profits they earned with his seed, he would give them their seed free of charge. (By 1966, the higher yield from hybrid seed accounted for one quarter of the total national corn crop.)

Wallace also carried on the family tradition of sharing ideas with the public. In 1920, he won praise for his book *Agricultural Prices*, the first economic analysis of its kind about farming. He also contributed frequently to the family business—the weekly *Wallace's Farmer.* When his father accepted the job of U.S. secretary of agriculture in Republican president Warren G. Harding's administration, Henry took over as editor of the paper.

For most of his early life, Wallace quietly supported Republican policies but remained uninvolved in politics. Like his father and grandfather, however, Wallace enthusiastically supported presidential candidate Theodore Roosevelt of the Progressive Party in 1912. But as time went on, Wallace's studies convinced him that the unregulated free enterprise system was driving farmers out of business. Moreover, he did not think that either Republicans or Democrats were doing much to help the situation. Thus, Wallace encouraged farmers to join together to gain a larger voice in political affairs. He supported policies such as federal crop insurance, low tariffs, and international cooperation to expand agricultural markets.

When the Republicans opposed these policies, Wallace supported their opponents. In his 1924 columns for *Wallace's Farmer*, Wallace criticized Republican president Calvin Coolidge and urged readers to vote for third-party candidate Robert M. La Follette instead.

Although Wallace was still registered as a Republican (he neglected to change his party affiliation until 1936), he threw his support to Democratic candidates Al Smith in 1928 and Franklin Roosevelt in 1932. Roosevelt, who won the presidential election in 1932, was so impressed by Wallace's columns that he asked the Iowa farmer to serve as the U.S. secretary of agriculture. Wallace brought his work ethic to the job. In his first year as a public official, Wallace visited almost every U.S. state and made about 100 speeches.

Wallace distinguished himself as no other secretary of agriculture had done. He helped push through the

Even though many people considered him shy, Henry A. Wallace spoke to crowds across the country during his years as a public official.

Rural Electrification Administration that brought inexpensive electricity to farms, and he installed a policy that paid farmers to plow under some of their crops to ease the surplus that was reducing farm prices. Although this policy went against his strongest beliefs, Wallace declared that these were "emergency acts made necessary by the almost insane lack of world statesmanship."

Wallace, in fact, proved to be such an able and intelligent administrator that Roosevelt selected him as his vice-presidential running mate in 1940. Once in office, however, the minimal duties of the vice-president bored Wallace, who complained he had little more to do than play tennis. But as World War II engulfed the United States, Roosevelt found important jobs for his vice-president. Wallace assumed leadership of the War Production Board that was responsible for overseeing the nation's economic output during the war crisis. He also chaired the Board of Economic Warfare, which dealt with U.S. foreign trade policy.

Wallace also used his new influence to spread his vision for the future. His experience as a plant breeder led him to view science as a limitless source of wealth. He foresaw a "Century of the Common Man," in which the nations of the world would share the overflow of riches with the poor and the powerless. Political leaders throughout the world had only to throw down trade barriers, stop exploiting other nations, and open their arms to international cooperation.

The idealistic Wallace, however, believed that maintaining peace demanded a world community linked by an organization like the United Nations. Wallace wanted to include everyone in his vision of the future. He wanted equal opportunities for minorities and for women, and he was one of the first supporters of the idea of national medical insurance.

Wallace's radical support for international government and labor groups and his criticisms of capitalism appalled many Democratic leaders. Even President Roosevelt feared that his vice-president's outspoken views could cause trouble in a reelection campaign. When Roosevelt ran for a fourth term in 1944, he dropped Wallace as his running mate. Roosevelt had accurately judged the hostility that Wallace had provoked. Following his 1944 victory, Roosevelt barely got Congress to approve Wallace as his secretary of commerce.

Had Roosevelt retained Wallace as his vice-president, Wallace would have taken over the presidency in 1945, when Roosevelt died in office. Instead, the responsibility went to Roosevelt's vice-president, Harry Truman. Wallace did not trust Truman. He was especially alarmed at the way the new president handled tensions between the United States and the Soviet Union following World War II.

Wallace called for a strong United Nations organization to enforce peace throughout the world, but Truman, and most Americans, preferred to trust the U.S.

While serving under President Franklin Roosevelt (1882-1945), Henry A. Wallace was secretary of agriculture from 1933 to 1940, vice-president from 1941 to 1945, and secretary of commerce in 1945.

military to enforce its policies. In contrast to those who believed in the strength of arms, Wallace said that a U.S. weapons build-up would only frighten and anger the Soviet Union into an even more warlike position. Such a build up, he argued, would divide the world into two major camps and pit the United States against the Soviets in a fight for world domination. Given the destructive force of the newly developed nuclear weapons, Wallace saw an arms build-up as a suicidal course.

Favoring a peaceful approach to the Soviets, Wallace was confident that the American free-enterprise system would show itself to be superior to the Soviet Union's communist system. This, he maintained, would force the Soviets to cooperate with the United States. "If an effort is made to get along peacefully, Russia might find a lot in the capitalistic system that could be of service to it," Wallace said.

Although Wallace tried to persuade Truman to his way of thinking, Wallace eventually recognized that the president was paying no attention to him. In September 1946, Wallace delivered a speech in New York City in which he spoke against Truman's policies. Within one week, Wallace resigned from his position as secretary of commerce.

The fear that Truman was leading the United States back to the edge of war continued to haunt Wallace. Someone had to try to stop the president and preach the message of peace—even against hopeless odds. On December 29, 1947, Wallace announced he would run for president in order to bring "real Americanism back again to the United States." He called his supporters "Gideon's Army," a biblical reference to an Israelite farmer who defeated the oppressive Midianite government that had ruled Israel for 40 years. Wallace believed that his supporters could overcome tremendous odds to save the United States from disaster.

Invoking the memory of former Progressive presidential candidates Theodore Roosevelt and Robert M. La Follette, Wallace organized a new Progressive Party.

Aside from their objections to Truman's "Cold War" policies that opposed communism and the Soviet Union, the Progressives declared that the "root cause of crisis is big business control of our economy and government." This new third party called for a minimum wage for workers, price supports for farmers, and an extensive old-age pension.

Supported by a core group of wealthy liberals, Wallace and his running mate, Idaho senator Glenn Taylor, enjoyed better financial backing than most third-party candidates. For a time, their campaign appeared to be growing in strength. But Wallace managed his campaign poorly. During all his years in Washington, D.C., he had learned very little about politics.

Idaho senator Glenn Taylor, who held office from 1945 to 1951, was officially still a Democrat in 1948, when he became the Progressive Party's vice-presidential candidate.

A 1948 campaign button for presidential candidate Henry A. Wallace

Wallace damaged his campaign by accepting the endorsement of the small American Communist Party. Most Americans considered Communists to be enemies of the United States. This view had increased with Josef Stalin's powerful communist dictatorship in the Soviet Union. But Wallace made no effort to distance himself from the Communists and told a reporter, "Anyone who will work for peace is okay with me." When it came to politics, he offered excuses for brutal Soviet actions such as the blockade of Berlin.

Politicians of all parties are often the subject of political cartoons, such as this caricature of Henry A. Wallace from the 1940s.

The press immediately attacked Wallace's views. *Newsweek* magazine reported that Wallace's "press conferences, newspaper statements, and radio addresses faithfully echoed the Communist party line." Wallace's support soon shrank like a leaky balloon. Wallace, whom Franklin Roosevelt had called "Old Man Common Sense," seemed to have lost his bearings.

In the 1948 election, Wallace collected fewer than 1.2 million votes, more than half of which were in the state of New York. Ironically, some of the domestic programs championed by Wallace and his Progressives, such as the minimum wage and farm price supports, became a reality in the decades that followed. But Wallace had failed in his most important campaign goal: to head off the Cold War hysteria or the expensive nuclear arms race between the United States and the Soviet Union.

Henry A. Wallace died on November 18, 1965, of amyotrophic lateral sclerosis, a rare form of spinal paralysis that is popularly known as Lou Gehrig's disease. At that time, the United States was caught in the controversial Vietnam War, one of the worst crises spawned by the Cold War.

More than 20 years after his death, Henry A. Wallace received some vindication when the failure of the Soviet Union's economic system ended the threat of Communist expansion in the world—just as he had predicted.

On September 14, 1948, the new States' Rights Party nominated South Carolina governor Strom Thurmond for president.

5

Strom Thurmond
The Dixiecrat

Democratic president Harry Truman walked into a heated political crossfire during the 1948 election. First, the liberal wing of his Democratic Party, upset by Truman's foreign policy, broke off and supported Progressive candidate Henry A. Wallace. Then, the conservatives, angered by Truman's domestic policy, walked out and formed *their* own party.

The move by the States' Rights Democrats, popularly known as "Dixiecrats" because of their concentration in the South, threatened to cost the divided Democrats the election. But the Dixiecrats were so incensed over Truman's civil rights stance that they were willing to torpedo the Democrats' election chances to make their point. In fact, the worse the Democrats did in the election, the stronger the Dixiecrats' chances of reforming the major party into one more favorable to their way of thinking.

The man the Dixiecrats chose to carry their banner was Strom Thurmond. The young, relatively unknown governor from South Carolina was as well-steeped in rough-and-tumble state politics as Henry A. Wallace was in agriculture. Thurmond's father, John, had been a local politician and an attorney and campaign manager for Ben Tillman—sometimes called "Pitchfork Ben"—South Carolina's outspokenly racist governor and senator. John Thurmond once shot a man to death in a quarrel over

During his 23 years as a senator and governor of South Carolina, Ben Tillman (1847-1918) supported the rights of farmers and argued that black people should not be allowed to vote.

Tillman's political views, pleading that the shooting was self-defense. Tillman later appointed him to be a U.S. attorney.

To help supplement his earnings as a lawyer, John Thurmond and his wife bought a farm in Edgefield, South Carolina, about 50 miles west of Columbia. One of their six children was future politician James Strom Thurmond, who was born on December 5, 1902.

While growing up, Strom spent much of his time working on the family farm. He attended the local schools and trained as a cross-country runner in his spare time. When he enrolled at Clemson University in 1918, he continued to run long distances and studied to become a teacher. After graduating in 1923, he taught for several years at small high schools in rural South Carolina. But Thurmond was not happy being a teacher, so he began taking law courses through a correspondence school. In December 1930, Thurmond passed the bar exam and joined his father's law firm.

Strom worked for a few years as a city and county attorney, then jumped into state politics. In 1933, he won election to the South Carolina state senate as a Democrat. A strong supporter of government aid to those who were struggling in society, Thurmond sponsored legislation giving assistance to the elderly, the blind, and to children living in poverty. He favored laws protecting farmers from economic ruin and voted to increase tax dollars for education.

Even though he gave up teaching to study law, Strom Thurmond had been called a "zealous instructor" by the Augusta Herald *newspaper in South Carolina, and he was widely respected by his students.*

In 1938, 35-year-old Thurmond became the youngest circuit judge in South Carolina. When the United States entered World War II in 1941, Thurmond left the bench to join the armed forces. He saw plenty of action, from the 1944 landing on the beaches of Normandy in Europe to battles against the Japanese in the Pacific. In January 1946, he returned home highly decorated for his efforts during the war.

Later that year, Thurmond declared himself a candidate for governor of South Carolina. His record as a war hero helped him to attract attention in a campaign crowded by ten other candidates. Thurmond won the election and set about trying to make South Carolina's state government more efficient. Still an educator at heart, he led a drive to boost public-school teachers' pay by 25 percent.

The new governor had been in office less than two years when the Democratic Party met for their 1948 convention. At this time, Thurmond had received virtually no national attention except for stirring up a bit of gossip by marrying Jean Crouch, a member of his office staff, in 1947. Her future husband had once selected her "Miss South Carolina" in a college beauty contest and, at age 21, she became the youngest First Lady in the history of South Carolina.

In the years following World War II, the United States took a hard look at its long-standing acceptance of discrimination against black citizens. At its 1948 national convention, the Democratic Party decided to come out strongly in favor of better treatment of blacks. The party's platform favored federal laws outlawing segregation in public places and called for a ban on the poll tax—the practice of charging a fee for the privilege of voting. (In the South, the poll tax was used to discourage blacks from voting.) These proposals infuriated some white Democrats from the South, who had been brought up in a segregated society and didn't want things to change.

These southern Democrats insisted that they were in favor of equal treatment for blacks, and they cited the record of politicians such as Strom Thurmond to prove this. Governor Thurmond had requested an increase in the amount of money spent for educating blacks and had ordered a special prosecutor to investigate the lynching of a black man.

While they were willing to take steps to increase the number of opportunities for blacks, many white southerners did not believe in racial integration; they were firmly against sharing schools and other public facilities with blacks. Above all, they resented the federal government dictating such laws to the states. Governor Thurmond, in fact, had argued for an end to the poll tax in South Carolina, but the idea of the federal government *ordering* them to end the tax infuriated the politicians in the state.

Some southerners at the convention charged that northern Democrats had pushed through the civil rights resolutions in an attempt to humiliate the South. Because mainline Democrats insisted on increased civil rights for blacks, the entire Mississippi delegation and half of the Alabama delegates walked out of the convention hall in protest.

Three days after the close of the convention, Governor Fielding Wright of Mississippi invited all Democrats who opposed the party's civil rights policy to meet in Birmingham, Alabama, to register their protest. This meeting attracted a large number of southern politicians who wanted to run their own candidate against President Harry Truman, the Democratic nominee.

At first, Thurmond opposed the idea of splitting from the Democratic Party. Although he was unhappy with many Democratic policies, Thurmond remained a committed Democrat. Like many southerners, he had a hard time forgiving the Republicans for their treatment of the South following the Civil War. Thurmond realized that the southern Democrats, or "Dixiecrats," had little hope of winning the election. By running a candidate, they would split the Democratic Party in half and inadvertently help to increase the Republicans' chances of winning.

But Thurmond also understood the depth of South Carolina's anger over the civil rights issue. When other

In 1948, Governor Strom Thurmond and other southern politicians thought that creating a new party would force other Democrats to be more attentive to the needs of the South.

southerners proposed him as their presidential candidate, he realized he had nothing to lose. Even if he ran a poor third or even fourth in the election, he would win the affection of South Carolina voters. With this in mind, Thurmond accepted the offer. On July 17, 1948, the southern Democrats unanimously selected Strom Thurmond as their candidate. Fielding Wright signed on as Thurmond's vice-presidential running mate on the States' Rights Party ticket.

In his campaign, Thurmond tried to defuse the charges of racism that the Democrats were leveling against the South. He stressed that the Dixiecrats' campaign was about states' rights, not about race. "I am not

Vice-presidential candidate Fielding Wright (1895-1956), who was governor of Mississippi from 1946 to 1955, said "true Democrats" would join the States' Rights Party and become "Dixiecrats."

This 1948 campaign button shows that members of the new States' Rights Party did not want to dissociate themselves entirely from the Democrats.

interested one whit in the question of white supremacy," he declared. Thurmond maintained his purpose was to stop the growing power of the federal government, which sought to control the actions of the states.

The actions of the federal government, said Thurmond, were not only dangerous but also illegal, since the U.S. Constitution stated that Congress had no authority to interfere with the business of the states. Thurmond linked the growth of the federal government to a growing Communist influence in the nation. He warned that the northern Democrats were setting up "a new kind of police state with all power centered in Washington." The Dixiecrats, according to Thurmond, were fighting for "the protection of the American people against the onward march of totalitarian government."

However, *Time* magazine charged that the "counterfeit argument for states' rights" was just a cover for a campaign to deny blacks their rights. The national magazine pointed out that for all the talk by southern politicians about their efforts to advance the cause of blacks, they had done nothing to break down the barriers of race that for so many years had stamped blacks as inferior people.

Both *Time* and Thurmond exaggerated. The issue of states' rights was intensely important to southerners and certainly motivated many Dixiecrat supporters. On the other hand, racial prejudice clearly provided much of the fuel that fired the Dixiecrats' campaign. Some whites openly welcomed the effort as a chance to "put niggers in their place."

Despite his denial that race was an issue, Thurmond increased racial unrest by accusing the other presidential candidates of "kowtowing to minority blocs." He appealed to white southern pride when he declared, "There's not enough troops in the Army . . . to break down segregation." He demonstrated his acceptance of the social barriers in the South by asking, "When will they [the federal government] learn, as the South has learned, that you can't legislate racial harmony?"

Thurmond and his supporters in the States' Rights Party had no illusions about gaining the White House and only a faint hope of winning enough votes to prevent either Truman or his Republican opponent, Thomas Dewey, from winning the election. Except for the core of southern states, the only state in which Thurmond's name appeared on the ballot was North Dakota. The Dixiecrats' main goal was simply to show the Democratic Party that it could not take the South for granted.

Political observers predicted that Thurmond's candidacy would dramatically drive home that point. Some people argued that Truman had made the biggest mistake of his political career when he assumed that the South would stand by idly while the Democrats adopted a strong civil rights platform. In fact, Thurmond stood a good chance of winning the southern states where

New York governor Thomas Dewey (1902-1971), who had earned a national reputation for his strong stance against crime, was the Republican Party's presidential candidate in 1944 and 1948.

Democratic candidates usually won elections without much of a fight. The probable Democratic loss of those states prompted *Newsweek* magazine to call the Dixiecrat movement "a political revolt that all but dooms the candidacy of Harry Truman."

With the Democrats in disarray, Republican nominee Thomas Dewey grew more confident. During the final days of the campaign, he was so certain that he would be president that he began spending more time campaigning for Republican congressional candidates than for himself. *Time* magazine agreed. Less than three weeks before the election, the magazine listed Dewey as the likely winner and predicted he would receive 350 electoral votes.

President Harry Truman, however, claimed not to be worried about the Dixiecrats. He believed that Progressive candidate Henry A. Wallace posed more of a threat than Thurmond. The president, however, turned out to be wrong about which third-party candidate was the stronger. True, Thurmond and Wallace each received a little more than 1 million votes, and neither attracted as much as three percent of the total vote. But because Thurmond's strength was concentrated in a smaller area, his supporters made a greater impact. Helped by the fact that Alabama, Louisiana, Mississippi, and South Carolina listed him as the candidate of the regular Democratic Party, Thurmond won each of those states and their 39 electoral votes.

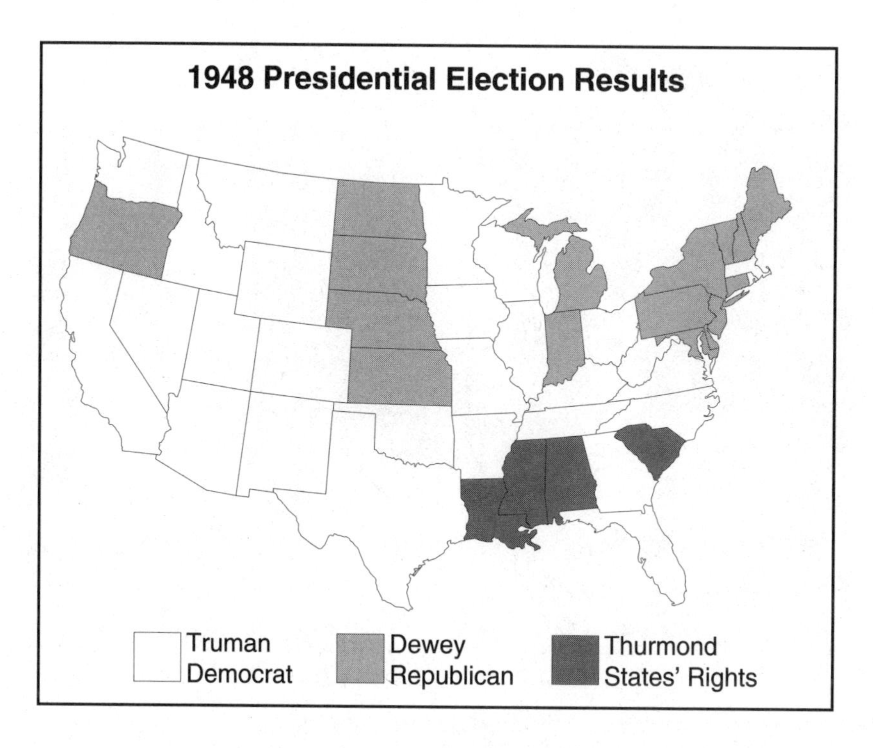

With 303 electoral votes, Democrat Harry Truman defeated Republican Thomas Dewey, who won 189 votes, and States' Rights candidate Strom Thurmond, who received 39.

But many political leaders in the South swallowed their indignation over the civil rights planks and supported the national Democratic Party. As a result, Thurmond captured no other states. Harry Truman survived the three-pronged attack on his presidency. The president trounced Republican Dewey by 2 million votes, and he won 303 electoral votes to Dewey's 189 electoral votes and Thurmond's 39. Progressive Henry A. Wallace received no electoral votes.

Harry Truman holds up an early edition of the November 4, 1948, Chicago Daily Tribune, *which inaccurately reported that Thomas Dewey had won the presidential election.*

The Dixiecrats' campaign for states' rights in the area of civil rights did not turn the tide of public opinion in their favor. Recognition of minority rights and the equality of races went forward in spite of them. The most important historical role that the Dixiecrats played was probably in shuffling the political deck in the South. During the campaign, reporters wondered if the Dixiecrat Party was a "political decompression chamber" for conservative Democrats who were fed up with their party and ready to join the Republicans.

Sure enough, conservative southern Democrats gradually defected to the Republican Party. One of the first to do that was Strom Thurmond, the States' Rights Party's only presidential candidate in history. In 1964, Thurmond switched his party allegiance and used his influence to help Barry Goldwater become the first Republican presidential candidate to carry South Carolina since 1876. Immensely popular in his home state, Thurmond has won every election he has ever entered since his 1948 run for the presidency.

In the mid-1990s, more than 45 years after he became the States' Right Party's candidate for president, Strom Thurmond continues to serve as the oldest member of the U.S. Senate.

Strom Thurmond was first elected to the U.S. Senate in 1954. He is now a member of the Judiciary, Armed Services, Labor and Human Resources, and Veterans' Affairs committees.

George Wallace, a leading opponent of the civil rights movement, won the support of many white southerners in 1968.

6

George Wallace
Just Plain Folks

On the surface, George Wallace's third-party presidential campaign appears to have been a rerun of Strom Thurmond's 1948 effort. Like Thurmond, Wallace was a southern Democratic governor who strongly favored segregation. Like the "Dixiecrat" Thurmond, Wallace ran for president against his party's chosen candidate on a platform of preserving states' rights.

While Thurmond's supporters had chosen him to represent the views of their new party, Wallace's backers formed a third party to help him express his views.

Without Thurmond, members of the States' Rights Party would have chosen someone else and achieved about the same results in the 1948 presidential election. But without Wallace, there would have been no American Independent Party.

A colorful national figure who inspired devotion in many and hatred in others, George Wallace burst onto the American political scene in a blaze of racist defiance. But he was more than a one-issue southern politician. Like many other third-party candidates, Wallace held a genuine affection for the common people and a dislike for the established powers of government.

Unlike many politicians, however, Wallace spoke about political issues in simple, blunt, and sometimes shocking terms. Wallace presented himself as the champion of "the workin' folks all over this country who are gettin' fed up and are gonna turn this country around."

George Corley Wallace Jr. was born in Clio, a small town in southeastern Alabama, on August 25, 1919. His mother, Mozelle Smith Wallace, taught music and home economics, while his father, George Sr., made a living renting out his three small farms to tenant farmers.

George Sr. loved politics, but his poor health prevented him from running for office. Instead, he spent much of his time helping others run their campaigns. He passed on this interest in politics to his son. A talkative boy, George Jr. enjoyed speaking with almost anyone, from close friends and family to strangers. At the age of nine, he contributed to his grandfather's successful campaign for probate judge. George Jr. said that waiting for the election returns was "the most exciting night of my life, being with the grownups and politicians until midnight."

At that time, the United States was mired in its worst economic depression. As George Wallace mingled among his neighbors in the country, he was struck by the grim lives many of them were living. Few people had much money, and some families clothed their children by making shirts out of feed sacks. Wallace saw dozens of people who were able and willing to work hard, but who could not find a job during those times of scarcity. Memories of those scenes stayed with George for the rest of his life.

George Wallace constantly felt drawn to do something to help people, especially those trapped by unfortunate circumstances. This philosophy conflicted with his views about blacks. He grew up in a culture that labeled blacks as inferior and tried to seal them off from white society. While Wallace accepted this attitude, as a circuit judge he would show great sympathy toward individual blacks who were victims of injustice. He earned a reputation for running a racially fair courtroom.

George was also tough enough to play quarterback on his high school football team despite being the smallest player on the field. Devoted to boxing, Wallace won Alabama's Golden Gloves bantamweight championships in 1936 and 1937. He and his two brothers started boxing as young boys because, as his brother Jack later recalled, "Daddy got tired of us fighting each other all the time, so he bought us gloves."

In high school, George also worked as a page, running errands for lawmakers in the Alabama state legislature. The job required him to live in a boarding house in Montgomery, the capital of Alabama. Wallace went on to attend the University of Alabama. A man of boundless energy, he was elected freshman class president, worked on several committees, held down part-time jobs, and continued his boxing. Somehow, he still managed to have time for his studies.

After graduating from college, George Wallace attended law school at the University of Alabama and received his law degree in 1942. During World War II, he joined the Army Air Corps pilot training program in Arkadelphia, Arkansas. There, he developed a severe case of spinal meningitis that threw him into a coma for six days and nearly killed him. The illness prevented him from completing his pilot training, so he instead served as a flight engineer on B-29 bombers over the Pacific Ocean. The many hours spent next to the shrieking engines left him with partial hearing loss.

After the war, Wallace returned to southeastern Alabama with his wife, Lurleen. By this time, he was ready to run for political office on his own. At age 27, Wallace was elected to the state legislature in 1946. He set about with his usual energy on what many considered a radical program in favor of the common people.

In the Alabama legislature, Wallace sponsored laws establishing social security pensions, junior colleges, and technical schools to help people train for careers. He also supported giving free tuition to the widows and children of men who had died fighting in the armed forces. Horrified by the state of the veterans hospital that treated his brother Gerald for tuberculosis, Wallace worked to improve such facilities throughout the state.

In 1952, Wallace was elected circuit judge of the Third Judicial District of Alabama. Judge Wallace ran an informal courtroom. When farmers appeared in court because they were in debt, Wallace often gave them legal advice about how they could best solve their financial problems.

In 1958, Wallace ran for governor in the Democratic primary. After losing by more than 60,000 votes, he joined his brother Gerald's law practice. But he did very little legal work because he had his eyes set on the next election. As one of his friends commented, "He ain't got but one serious appetite and that's votes." Wallace made speeches throughout the state and talked face to face with voters. His incredible memory for names and faces helped him to win the trust of voters, who believed Wallace was a man who understood them and their problems.

Wallace's folksy campaign paid off as he easily won Alabama's gubernatorial election in 1962. Never one to mask where he stood on the issues, he created an immediate national sensation with his inaugural speech. Answering the critics of the South who demanded the end of racial segregation, he thundered, "Segregation now! Segregation tomorrow! Segregation forever!"

That summer, a federal court order required that the all-white University of Alabama open its doors to black students. "I will never myself submit voluntarily to any integration of any school system in Alabama," Wallace said, and he backed up his words with actions. The governor personally blocked the doorway to prevent the first two black students from entering the university. When armed troops arrived four hours later to enforce the order, Wallace read a statement denouncing federal interference in state affairs and then stepped aside.

This dramatic stand at the university brought Wallace national attention. Those who admired his courage urged him to run for president in 1964 to oppose the civil rights laws making their way through Congress. Wallace entered the Democratic presidential primaries opposing Democratic president Lyndon Johnson. Unlike the southern Dixiecrats of 1948, Wallace took his straight-talking, no-nonsense campaign to the North.

Wallace ran into passionate opposition in many places across the nation. At one college campus, 50 angry students tried to tip over his car. Nevertheless, Wallace

George Wallace (right) blocks a doorway at the University of Alabama—his alma mater—to prevent black students from entering.

Unlike George Wallace, President Lyndon Johnson (1908-1973) strongly supported desegregation and the civil rights movement.

triggered a large voter backlash against civil rights advances. Although he did not come close to defeating Johnson for the nomination, Wallace won 35 percent of the votes in the Democratic primary in Wisconsin, nearly 30 percent in Indiana, and came close to winning Maryland, with 45 percent of the votes in that state.

The Alabama state constitution did not allow the governor to run for a second consecutive term of office. In 1966, as Wallace's four-year term drew to a close, he tried to persuade Alabama lawmakers to bring before the voters an amendment that would allow him to stay in office. When the legislature refused, Wallace's wife, Lurleen, ran in his place and won the election. Although Lurleen took an active role in governing the state, her position allowed George to stay involved in politics.

When term limits prevented George Wallace from running again for governor in 1966, his wife, Lurleen Wallace (1926-1968), was elected to take his place.

During the 1960s, sweeping civil rights changes, an explosion of black anger in the inner cities, and violent protests against the Vietnam War frightened and angered many white Americans. Resisting change, these citizens longed for the security they had known while growing up.

George Wallace was one of the few politicians who boldly said what these people were thinking. He scored points with many working-class people by ridiculing the "pointy-headed intellectuals," whom he said were destroying America with their half-baked theories of social change. He saved special scorn for Earl Warren, the chief justice of the U.S. Supreme Court. Warren had spearheaded the federal courts' orders for school desegregation and decisions that increased the rights of

As chief justice of the Supreme Court from 1953 to 1969, Earl Warren (1891-1974) became known for supporting the rights of minorities and poor people.

people suspected of committing crimes. According to Wallace, Warren didn't have "enough brains in his whole head to try a chicken thief in Chilton County."

Wallace's no-nonsense, plain-talking style attracted a large number of enthusiastic supporters. As one reporter said, "You can't help but respond to him. He made those people feel something real for once in their lives." On the other hand, his intemperate remarks, especially on race relations, earned him many bitter enemies.

Seeing himself as the only voice of ordinary people in national politics, Wallace decided to make another try for the presidency in 1968. Recognizing that his odds of winning the Democratic nomination were slim, and convinced that the Republicans were no more capable of governing than the Democrats, Wallace chose to run as a third-party candidate. His supporters formed the American Independent Party as an alternative to the Democrats and the Republicans.

According to the American Independent Party platform, the party's goal was to "return this country to its accustomed and deserved position of leadership among the community of nations and to offer hope to our people of some relief from the continued turmoil, frustration, and confusion brought about through the fearful and inept leadership of our national political leaders." For its vice-presidential candidate, the party selected retired Air Force general Curtis LeMay, a blunt critic of Americans who were protesting the Vietnam War.

Curtis LeMay (1906-1990), George Wallace's 1968 running mate, had been the U.S. Air Force's chief of staff from 1961 to 1965.

Grief nearly put an end to Wallace's candidacy just as it was getting started. After his wife, Lurleen, died of cancer on May 7, 1968, Wallace fell into a depression for several months. But he pulled himself together and embarked on a furious campaign, flying around the country in a four-propeller airplane.

Wherever he traveled, Wallace sounded the old Dixiecrat warning about the growing power of the federal government. He promised to reduce federal interference so that ordinary people could make their own decisions on how they wanted to live. Hammering hard on basic conservative themes, Wallace maintained that, if elected, he would cut taxes, reduce crime by adding more law enforcement officers and establishing tougher penalties for criminals, and use greater force to achieve a military victory in Vietnam.

Wallace's distrust of the Soviet Union also pleased his conservative supporters. Still, his desire to help the common people also prompted him to advocate some liberal programs, such as aid to the elderly, price supports for farmers, a fair minimum wage, and new low-cost mass transit systems.

Wallace's fiery speeches, along with his frequent clashes with reporters and hecklers, helped him to attract far more attention than most third-party candidates. In fact, he gained such widespread support that his American Independent Party qualified for the ballot in all 50 states.

With Republican Richard Nixon and Democrat Hubert Humphrey running neck-and-neck in the 1968 campaign, Wallace had a good shot at denying either of them a clear-cut victory. He far exceeded the 1948 Dixiecrat showing by capturing nearly 9.5 million votes, which was more than 13 percent of the total cast. He finished first in three of the states that had voted for Dixiecrat Strom Thurmond in 1948—Alabama, Louisiana, and Mississippi—plus Arkansas and Georgia. Nixon was able to gain enough electoral votes to claim the presidency.

Having demonstrated that he represented a formidable bloc of voters, Wallace returned to the Democratic

Democrat Hubert Humphrey (1911-1978) and Republican Richard Nixon (1913-1994) were the two major candidates in the 1968 presidential election.

Party. When Alabamans sent him back to the governor's mansion in 1971, Wallace again set out to capture the Democratic nomination for president. This time he believed he had a realistic shot at winning. "Send them a message," his campaign slogan urged.

In the Florida primary, Wallace showed he was a force to be reckoned with. He collected 42 percent of the vote in a convincing win over ten other candidates. *Time* magazine called this success "the greatest victory of his turbulent life."

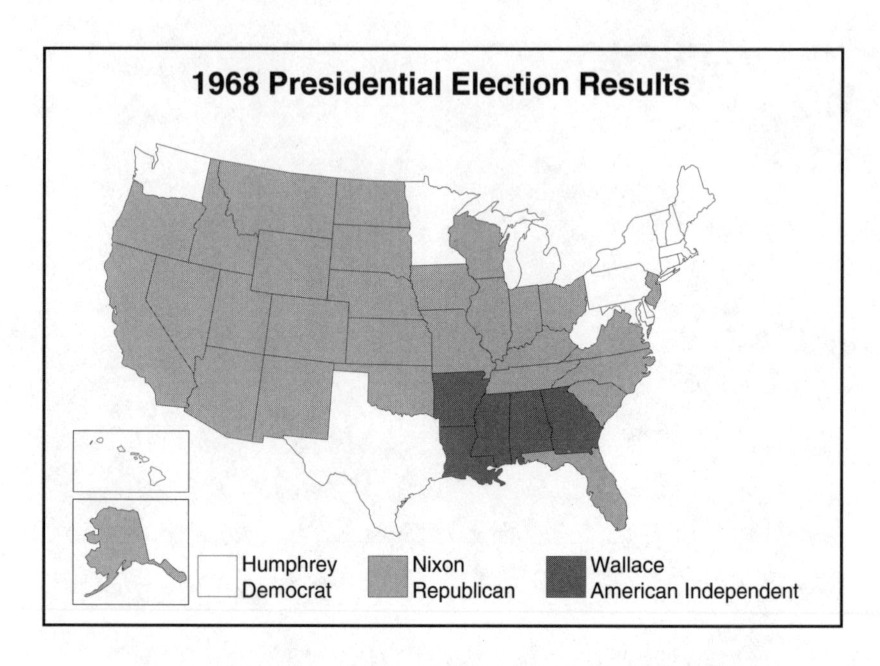

In 1968, Republican Richard Nixon was elected president with 301 electoral votes. Democrat Hubert Humphrey won 191 electoral votes, and American Independent candidate George Wallace received 46.

Although George Wallace gradually downplayed the segregationist stance from earlier in his career, he could not shed his reputation as a symbol of racism. Because of the hostility Wallace provoked in the eyes of much of the public, many of his friends expressed the fear that someone would try to kill him. "If it takes that to change the direction of this country," Wallace insisted, "it will take that."

An assassination attempt came in May during the 1972 campaign. As Wallace was shaking hands with shoppers outside a mall in Laurel, Maryland, a man named Arthur Bremer—who had been following Wallace from city to city—fired five shots at him with a .38 caliber pistol. At least four of the bullets struck Wallace. One injured his spine and left him paralyzed from the waist down.

Even though his supporters begged him to continue to seek the presidency, Wallace declined because he was suffering constantly from pain. He continued as Alabama's governor from 1971 until 1979. After taking some time off from politics, he again served as governor from 1982 to 1987.

Although George Wallace fell short of being a decisive factor in the presidential elections of 1964, 1968, and 1972, he did succeed in "sending them a message." Wallace gave voice to the fears of many Americans over the growing influence of the federal government and the speed of change in U.S. society. Those themes took root among enough people to carry conservative Republican candidate Ronald Reagan to the White House in 1980.

Illinois congressman John Anderson said he decided to run for president to give the public another choice.

7

John Anderson
The Uncandidate

Technically speaking, presidential candidate John Anderson wasn't a third-party candidate because he never officially joined a "third" party. That distinction aside, Anderson—who billed himself as an "independent"—made a fascinating run for the presidency in 1980 and got on the ballot precisely by defying the usual rules that apply to presidential candidates.

For most of the 1980 campaign, Anderson did not run like a person seriously interested in being elected to office. He entered a national election despite the fact that few Americans outside his home congressional district had ever heard of him. He swam upstream against the growing conservative forces in his party by running as a liberal Republican.

At a time when the press accused politicians of saying anything just to win votes, Anderson almost seemed to go out of his way to antagonize voters. For instance, he made an unpopular gasoline tax the cornerstone of his economic program, and decided to appear before a group of gun owners to declare his support for gun-control measures. When asked about some of his unpopular stands on issues, he said simply, "There are worse things than not being elected."

John Anderson ran for president not because he was obsessed with being elected, but rather to give the nation another choice. He had no confidence in the leadership abilities of Democratic president Jimmy Carter or Republican challenger Ronald Reagan. So many Americans had expressed their dismay at choosing between those two candidates that Anderson felt compelled to present himself as the "ideas candidate."

Born on February 15, 1922, in Rockford, Illinois, John Bayard Anderson was one of six children born to E. Albin Anderson, a Swedish immigrant, and his wife, Martha. The Andersons operated a small grocery store, which provided them with a middle-class income. They liked to attend large, religious tent meetings, and it was at one of those meetings that young John Anderson committed himself to living a Christian life. Following this experience, he decided to attend a seminary and become a preacher.

Eventually, however, John shifted his sights to the legal profession, where his skills as a student and a debater would serve him well. In 1939, he graduated first in his class from Rockford Central High School. He received his bachelor's degree from the University of Illinois in three years, then enrolled in the university's law school.

World War II interrupted John Anderson's legal studies. He spent more than two years in the army field artillery, earning four battle stars while serving in Europe. When he returned home, Anderson completed his law degree. He worked at a Rockford law firm for two years, then went on to graduate school at Harvard University.

After completing his studies in 1949, Anderson practiced law in Rockford for three years. In 1952, he got his first taste of government work when he went to Berlin, West Germany, as a diplomatic adviser in the foreign service. He married Keke Machakos, a young woman from Boston, and they returned to Rockford in 1955. The following year, some local Republicans asked Anderson to run for the office of district attorney of Winnebago County. Anderson accepted the challenge and won a hard-fought campaign.

In 1960, Anderson decided to run for the U.S. House of Representatives. At the start of the campaign, his name was unfamiliar to most voters in his district.

Nevertheless, Anderson swam against the current public opinion, as he would do much of his life. In a year when the Democrats—with the election of President John F. Kennedy—would regain control of the White House, John Anderson ran as a conservative Republican and won a seat in the U.S. Congress.

While in Washington, D.C., Anderson gained a reputation as one of the most conservative members of the House of Representatives. He fought against many of Kennedy's programs, especially social-action proposals such as Medicare, food stamps, and aid for mass transit. In 1964, he supported Republican presidential candidate Barry Goldwater, whom the nation overwhelmingly rejected. But the people in Anderson's traditionally Republican district agreed with Anderson's views and kept returning him to Congress.

In the mid-1960s, Anderson underwent a startling political transformation and began to vote in favor of many federal social policies. By 1968, when he had reached his fourth term in the House of Representatives, Anderson had become the chairman of the House Republican Conference, the third most powerful Republican post in Congress. That year, after initially opposing a law that would make it illegal for property owners to refuse to rent or sell their property to people on the basis of race, color, or belief, Anderson delivered an inspiring speech in support of the proposal. Political analysts gave him a large share of the credit for the ultimate passage of the legislation.

Formerly a strong supporter of defense, Anderson now began speaking out against the billions of dollars the country was throwing into a nuclear weapons race against the Soviet Union. Anderson saw many crucial needs that Americans could not address because the military was draining the federal treasury.

"It does little good to be armed to the teeth to deter external threats," Anderson said, "if we are not able to cope with the internal threats." In 1969, he urged his colleagues to end the arms race, which he called "this insane nuclear version of keeping up with the Joneses." The Illinois congressman explained his shift on this and other issues by saying, "You acquire more knowledge, you study new ideas, you recognize change, you grow."

Despite his change in viewpoint, Anderson continued to support the leadership of the Republican Party, particularly President Richard Nixon, who won the 1968 election. Still, Anderson split with Republicans on many issues and urged the Republicans to prove they could show compassion as well as balance a checkbook.

During the 1970s, Anderson took an increasingly dim view of U.S. military involvement in Vietnam. When word leaked out that members of the Nixon campaign organization had burglarized the Democrats' Watergate headquarters, Anderson was one of the first Republicans to demand an investigation.

On issues ranging from women's rights to gun control, Anderson continued to disagree with the leadership of his party. This independence cost Anderson the support of some Republicans, but most of his colleagues still respected his intelligence, honesty, and persuasiveness.

Anderson did his most effective work on the floor of Congress, rather than in front of the media. Because of this, few people noticed when he declared himself a candidate for the Republican presidential nomination on June 8, 1979. Anderson realized he was not a household name and that his chances of winning the nomination were slim at best. But he was about to retire from Congress and wanted "to get it all off my chest before I close up the books."

This new presidential candidate did not rigidly subscribe to a particular political point of view. "My heart is on the left and my pocketbook is on the right," he said, meaning that he tended to be liberal in caring about other people but conservative about spending money. Still, he tried to avoid political labels. "I don't care whether you call me a conservative or a liberal, so long as you give me credit for having ideas," he said.

In his campaign, Anderson boldly put forth unpopular plans that he was convinced the country needed. While this looked like political suicide to many observers, Anderson viewed it as a challenge. "I've learned what a pure joy it becomes to take an idea that tends to be unpopular and find a great number of people you can

John Anderson campaigns with his children, John Jr. (far left) and Eleanora (far right).

turn to your cause," he explained. Most important among his proposals was an energy conservation policy built around a 50-cent-per-gallon federal gasoline tax to be balanced by a 50 percent cut in Social Security taxes.

During the spring primaries of 1980, Anderson's forthright stands on the issues began to attract attention. College students in particular found his approach refreshing and supported him enthusiastically. The dignified, white-haired Anderson playfully accepted his role as the unlikely hero of the younger generation. He addressed college crowds as "My fellow Anderson freaks."

Anderson's campaign rose rapidly from an almost invisible effort to a genuine threat to the Democratic and Republican Parties. In the Vermont primary, he lost to

Ronald Reagan by only 29 percent to 30. In Massachusetts, Anderson defeated Reagan—31 percent to 29 percent. But Reagan's campaign gained momentum, and he even won in Anderson's state of Illinois. By April, Reagan had captured enough convention delegates to win the Republican nomination.

Because numerous voters were dissatisfied with the choice between Reagan and President Jimmy Carter, Anderson stayed in the race as an independent candidate. However, he did not officially organize a new party, and his National Unity campaign held no convention. His sole reason for running was that "our nation needs a choice in November."

While campaigning, Anderson told Americans to reject the simple solutions and the fluffy generalities of the major political parties. Instead, he sought to eliminate

Former Georgia governor Jimmy Carter, who had been elected president in 1976, was called a weak president by his political opponents.

the labels that pitted one group of Americans so solidly against another that neither could govern effectively. "We are all liberals; we are all conservatives," he declared.

Anderson's campaign prescribed a detailed plan for strengthening the economy. He called for tax reforms, along with policies that would reduce inflation and enable people to save more money. He favored cutting federal spending to 20 percent of the previous year's gross national product.

Above all, Anderson thought the president of the United States should be a problem solver who could be flexible enough to approach different issues in different ways. The National Unity platform stated, "In responding to the challenges we face, government must be frankly experimental in some fields, conventional in others. It must also be utterly ruthless in judging its performance and pruning its failures."

Late in the spring of 1980, political polls measured Anderson's support at more than 20 percent of likely voters. Former president Gerald Ford warned that Anderson's campaign could deny both Carter and Reagan victory and might force the House of Representatives to decide the winner of the election.

But the odds against the 58-year-old congressman were overwhelming. He had to spend most of his time and money fulfilling the requirements for his name to appear on the ballots in all 50 states, and he had to borrow funds just to run a minimal campaign. Moreover,

President Jimmy Carter refused to appear on national television with Anderson. Although Anderson did debate Reagan in September, Carter's unwillingness to participate took legitimacy away from Anderson's candidacy. Only 44 percent of the electorate viewed the Anderson-Reagan debate, compared with the 83 percent who watched the Carter-Reagan debate, which took place one week before the election.

Anderson had been unable to persuade any well-known political leaders to become his running mate and instead chose Patrick Lucey, a retired Wisconsin governor and former ambassador to Mexico. A Democrat, Lucey had previously supported another 1980 presidential hopeful, Senator Ted Kennedy of Massachusetts. Lucey had resigned as a delegate to the Democratic

Patrick Lucey, who had been Wisconsin's governor from 1971 to 1979, came out of retirement to become John Anderson's running mate on the National Unity ticket.

convention in August to protest incumbent President Jimmy Carter's renomination.

As Anderson's support began to falter, more of his backers abandoned him because they did not want to "waste" a vote on someone with almost no chance of winning. Anderson's support dwindled steadily until election day.

He finished with 5.7 million votes, about 7 percent of the total cast. He carried no states and was not a significant factor in the election, which Reagan won by a wide margin. Despite his promising start, Anderson's main contribution to the 1980 election campaign was reduced to simply providing an outlet for nearly 6 million voters to vent their dissatisfaction with the quality of the candidates on the ballot.

President Ronald Reagan, who held office from 1981 to 1989, was often called "the great communicator" because of his ability to win the public's trust.

Billionaire Ross Perot said he would run for president in 1992 . . . if the public insisted.

8

Ross Perot
The Super Salesman

Of all the third-party candidates who have run for president since Theodore Roosevelt in 1912, only Ross Perot had a real chance of winning the presidency. Perot could have written a book on the art of persuasion. He combined the blunt, folksy style of 1968 American Independent candidate George Wallace with the eccentric independence of 1980 National Unity candidate John Anderson. Perot ran as a "can do" business tycoon against two unpopular major party candidates at a time when public confidence in politicians had sunk to low levels.

Ross Perot said he could solve the nation's problems by working with the American people—but it would require sacrifice.

Most importantly, Perot turned the problem of campaign finances to his advantage. While most third-party candidates have had to struggle along on a shoestring budget, billionaire Perot outspent both the Republicans and Democrats—and hardly felt the pinch. During his 1992 campaign, Perot spent a total of $60 million—$23.9 million of that total on television advertising, compared with the $18.1 million spent by Republican president George Bush and the $9.4 million spent by Democratic challenger Bill Clinton.

The future presidential candidate was born Henry Ray Perot on June 27, 1930, in Texarkana, a city that straddles the border between Texas and Arkansas. He was the third child of Lulu May and Gabriel Ross Perot.

At the age of 12, he legally changed his name to Henry Ross Perot in an effort to ease his father's grief over the childhood death of Henry's older brother, Gabriel Ross Perot Jr. Along with the new name, Ross (as young Henry preferred to be called) accepted the responsibility of making his father as proud of him as possible.

While growing up during the Great Depression, Henry Ross Perot learned thriftiness from his father, a successful cotton broker who drove the same Dodge automobile for 20 years. He learned generosity from his mother, who often fed transient, homeless men who knocked on her door. Lulu Perot also lectured Ross sternly about morals and responsibility.

Ross grew comfortable with discipline while attending Patty Hill, a strict private school that taught ballroom dancing and opera as well as the regular curriculum. But even though he was more privileged than most people his age, Perot learned to make his own way in the world. He demonstrated his business talents by offering to deliver the *Texas Gazette* to the roughest and poorest section of Texarkana in exchange for much higher wages than most paper carriers earned. Perot then delivered the papers on horseback and by bicycle to keep a step ahead of robbers.

Through most of his school years, Perot achieved only average grades. But once he set his mind to something, he went after it with a bulldog tenacity. For instance, Perot gained his Eagle Scout badge—an honor that most Boy Scouts earn in three to five years—in only 16 months. After a high school teacher told him he was not very bright, Perot started bringing home A's.

Dreaming of becoming a lawyer, Perot attended the local junior college in Texarkana. A good leader and a skilled debater, he was elected as president of his class. When the U.S. Naval Academy accepted him in 1949, the patriotic Perot enthusiastically tossed aside his legal plans. Over the years, Perot has said that the academy gave him his first look at government waste. Officials issued him two pairs of shoes when he arrived at the academy, but Perot did not understand why anyone needed more than one pair.

Though only an average student at the academy, Perot again demonstrated his leadership ability. His class voted him the best all-around midshipman and class president. While at the academy, Perot also impressed a date named Margot Birmingham, who eventually married him. After graduating in 1953, Perot set sail on a destroyer to join the American war effort in Korea. He never saw fighting, however, because the opposing forces ceased hostilities before he arrived in Asia.

As a condition of attending the academy, Perot owed the navy at least five years of active service. Despite his apparent success in the navy, Perot asked to be relieved of active duty after only two years. Over the years, Perot has given different explanations for wanting to leave the navy, ranging from disgust at his shipmates' lack of morals to impatience with the military's seniority system that rewarded people on their length of service rather than on their performance.

In 1955, Perot's superiors ultimately transferred him to the aircraft carrier *Leyte*. While serving aboard this vessel, Perot's leadership skills earned him the privilege of escorting visitors around the ship. One of these visitors was an executive from a growing company called International Business Machines (IBM), which manufactured and sold computers. Perot had learned some basic computer skills aboard the *Leyte* and impressed the visitor, who suggested that Perot look him up when his tour of duty was over.

When he left the navy in 1957, Perot took the visitor up on his offer and joined the IBM office in Dallas, Texas. While his wife, Margot, taught fourth grade, Perot began working as a computer salesman. He charmed his clients with his polite, down-to-earth personality and his reliable performance. Before long, he was making more money on commissions than his bosses were earning in salary. In an attempt to equalize the earnings of employees, the Dallas office set a limit on the amount of commission a salesperson could earn in a year. In 1962, Perot reached his maximum yearly earnings in just three weeks!

Unwilling to sit around doing nothing for a year and irritated with the company's policy, Perot decided to take a chance on starting his own business. During his years at IBM, he had noticed that many companies leased IBM hardware without knowing how to use it. These companies wasted a great deal of time trying to learn how to operate the equipment and adapt it to meet their needs. Instead of producing computers, Perot decided to provide clients with the computer services they needed.

With this idea in mind, Perot established Electronic Data Systems (EDS) in 1962. He installed his own set of policies for his company, including a dress code and a moral code. A great believer in rewarding efficiency and performance, he gave employees huge financial incentives to trim costs and increase the company's profits.

Perot's big break came when he landed a large contract from Texas Blue Cross, a health insurance company. By 1965, new federal Medicare programs had produced an avalanche of paperwork that administrators could not process without computers. Perot's profits exploded from $26,000 in 1965 to roughly $2.4 million in 1968. When he offered the public a chance to buy stock in EDS, buyers responded so enthusiastically that Perot made more than $200 million in a single day. *Fortune* magazine called him "the fastest, richest Texan ever."

Claiming that "the day I made Eagle Scout was more important to me than the day I discovered I was a billionaire," Perot donated much of his wealth to worthy causes. He created a foundation that donated more than $100 million to schools, hospitals, and cultural organizations. If an employee developed health problems, Perot would get the best medical help in the country for the person and pay the bill himself. He retained a special spot in his heart for those in the armed forces: Whenever he saw someone in uniform at a restaurant, he insisted on paying for that person's meal.

Perot's strong patriotic feelings led him to take an active role in politics. In 1969, he ran newspaper and television ads totaling nearly $1 million in support of the U.S. war effort in Vietnam, which he saw as necessary to fight the spread of communism. That Christmas, he tried to deliver 30 tons of food, medicine, mail, and other gifts to U.S. prisoners of war being held in North Vietnam. This Communist country, however, refused to let the planes land. Perot tried again at Christmas in 1970, but the Soviet airliner he had chartered cancelled the flight. Nevertheless, the U.S. prisoners credited Perot's highly publicized efforts with embarrassing the North Vietnamese into improving their prison conditions.

A bold rescue mission in 1979 reinforced Perot's reputation as a man of action. Iranian police had arrested and illegally jailed two EDS employees who were working in Iran. When diplomatic efforts to free the employees failed, Perot sprang into action. "I just couldn't leave my people there to die," he said. Perot organized a commando squad and flew them into Tehran, where they helped to rescue the employees and fly them safely home.

In 1984, Perot sold his interest in EDS to General Motors Corporation for $2.55 billion. He was now an incredibly wealthy man of action with nothing to do. For a time, he focused on rooting out information about U.S. soldiers missing in action in Vietnam. Friends and admirers repeatedly suggested that he run for public office and use his considerable skills to retool an inefficient government. For years, Perot shrugged off the notion. "I wouldn't run for dogcatcher," he insisted.

As the economy of the United States slumped toward the beginning of 1992, Perot began to consider seriously the arguments in the many letters he had received. He finally decided that, as much as he hated politics, the country needed him to clean up the mess that its politicians had created. While appearing on the "Larry King Live" television show on February 20, 1992, Perot initially denied having any intention of running for president. But he hedged. If enough people wanted him to run, and if they could get him on the ballot in all 50 states and send in a small contribution to show their commitment, then he would not say no to them.

Many voters were unimpressed with the roster of candidates running for the Republican and Democratic nominations and responded to Perot. The U.S. government was broken, he declared, and the time had come for politicians to quit all their fancy talking and do something about fixing it.

Perot promised to bring to the government those qualities that had helped him earn his fortune. First, he said he would "clean out the barn" by cutting layers of

Ross Perot appears on "Larry King Live" with his wife, Margot (front, right), and their children (back row, left to right), Caroline, Ross Jr., and Nancy.

bureaucracy that wasted money and stopped things from getting done. Next, he would end the petty bickering between Democrats and Republicans by appointing the best people for the job, regardless of their party affiliation.

Finally, he would reward initiative and hard work in government and put "everybody who's breathing" back to work. If the American people elected him to office, Perot said, he would involve them more closely in decision making through an "electronic town hall," a vast information network that would discuss issues and tabulate the opinions of the citizens of the United States.

In the beginning, Perot aimed most of his campaign fire at Republican president George Bush, whom he accused of dragging his feet in investigating reports of U.S. soldiers still being held as prisoners in Vietnam. According to Perot, Bush was out of touch with the American public. "He didn't know there was a recession when millions of his own people were suffering," the billionaire said. Perot even tackled Bush on the president's strongest issue—the Persian Gulf War of 1991. "I don't

After serving as vice-president for eight years, George Bush was elected president in 1988. But Ross Perot and his supporters said President Bush failed to grasp the problems that most Americans faced.

have to prove my manhood by sending anybody to war," this third-party candidate said.

Above all, Perot stressed the dangers of the multi-trillion dollar deficit the nation was running. He urged Americans to face up to the responsibility of paying off this debt rather than leaving it as a burden on their children. The U.S. government either had to cut spending or raise taxes, he insisted, and if the voters "didn't have the stomach" to do what was right, they should not vote for him. Newspapers often described Perot as a "populist" because—despite his power in the world of business—he seemed to understand the problems and concerns of ordinary Americans.

With the American public's distrust of politicians running high, Perot—who was not a professional politician and who had millions of dollars at his disposal—posed a serious threat to the major political parties. A national poll taken in June 1992 showed Perot running ahead of the field with 37 percent to 33 for Republican incumbent Bush and 25 for Democratic challenger Clinton. When asked about Perot's chances of winning, former president Richard Nixon said, "I wouldn't bet against him."

Perot began to run into trouble, however, with his vague promises to repair the government. Voters wanted to know what specific plans he had and where he stood on the issues. But Perot declined to get into specifics, and critics pointed out some hypocrisy in his campaign. Perot had built a fortune from government spending on Medicare, yet he was running as the champion of those who were against such spending. Reports also leaked out about Perot's mean-spirited habit of hiring investigators to look into the lives of people he distrusted.

In July 1992, Perot rocked the political world by suddenly bowing out of the presidential race without any clear explanation. After demoralizing his supporters by withdrawing, Perot just as suddenly jumped back into the race in the autumn of 1992. At that time, he revealed that he had dropped out to protect his daughter Caroline from a Republican plot to disrupt her wedding. Perot offered no proof of the plot, and the bizarre explanation fueled opponents' claims that Perot was dangerously unstable.

The wealthy Texan scored well in debates with President Bush and Democratic challenger Clinton, the governor of Arkansas. More than half a foot shorter than his rivals and, by his own admission, "not much to look at," Perot often poked fun at himself and developed an informal public persona. Referring to perhaps his most prominent physical features, he said that if anyone had any good suggestions, he "was all ears!" Perot used humor and his colorful Texas accent to puncture the stiff formality of his opponents. In criticizing a proposed trade agreement with Mexico, Perot said, "that giant sucking sound you hear is American jobs going south."

President George Bush (center), First Lady Barbara Bush, and challengers Bill Clinton (left) and Ross Perot shake hands with the moderators following the presidential debate on October 12, 1992.

But Perot's running mate, James Stockdale, erased much of Perot's gains. A retired vice admiral who was held prisoner in Vietnam for seven years, Stockdale's credentials as a scholar and teacher were impressive, but his performance in the vice-presidential debates was painfully inept. As the campaign wound down, the momentum swung to Governor Clinton.

Perot launched a last-minute, multi-million-dollar television blitz to influence voters. He paid for several

Ross Perot's running mate, James Stockdale, shown here during the 1992 vice-presidential debate in Atlanta

lengthy television spots to discuss his plans for the United States and illustrate his opponents' weaknesses. Using numerous pie charts and graphs to illustrate his points, Perot painted Clinton as an inept leader of the small state of Arkansas who lacked the experience to take on the serious problems of the nation.

Perot, however, failed in his efforts to wrest the presidency from Clinton, who won the election despite capturing only 43 percent of the popular vote. Perot did not win a single state. However, he ran well in all areas of the country and attracted nearly 20 million votes. Perot won about 19 percent of the popular vote—the biggest share received by any third-party candidate since Theodore Roosevelt's 27.4 percent in 1912. By winning almost 20 million votes, Perot helped to show the depth of voter dissatisfaction with the country's political leaders.

Even more importantly, Perot got the attention of the two major parties and forced them to focus on the issues. Prior to Perot's entry into the race, neither major party candidate made a serious effort to address the nation's deficit problem. Once Perot jumped in, deficit reduction became one of the main issues. His third-party candidacy served as a warning that voters wanted action, not talk; results, not promises. Both Republicans and Democrats went about the job of governing with one eye on that formidable group of voters that Perot had organized.

Despite criticism that he lacked the experience to run the nation, Arkansas governor Bill Clinton was elected president in 1992.

The presidential seal of the United States of America

U.S. Presidential Election Results

The name of the person elected president appears at the top of each set of candidates.

Presidential Candidates	Political Party	Electoral Votes	Popular Votes*
1789			
George Washington	No party designations	69	
John Adams		34	
Other candidates		*35*	
Votes not cast		*8*	
1792			
George Washington	Federalist	132	
John Adams	Federalist	77	
George Clinton	Anti-Federalist	50	
Thomas Jefferson	Anti-Federalist	4	
Aaron Burr	Anti-Federalist	1	
Votes not cast		*6*	
1796			
John Adams	Federalist	71	
Thomas Jefferson	Democratic-Republican	68	
Thomas Pinckney	Federalist	59	
Aaron Burr	Democratic-Republican	30	
Other candidates		*48*	
1800			
Thomas Jefferson	Democratic-Republican	73	
Aaron Burr	Democratic-Republican	73	
John Adams	Federalist	65	
Charles C. Pinckney	Federalist	64	
John Jay	Federalist	1	

** Information about the number of popular votes each candidate received is not available for the presidential elections prior to 1872.*

1804

Thomas Jefferson	Democratic-Republican	162
Charles C. Pinckney	Federalist	14

1808

James Madison	Democratic-Republican	122
Charles C. Pinckney	Federalist	47
George Clinton	Democratic-Republican	6
Votes not cast		*1*

1812

James Madison	Democratic-Republican	128
DeWitt Clinton	Federalist	89
Votes not cast		*1*

1816

James Monroe	Democratic-Republican	183
Rufus King	Federalist	34
Votes not cast		*4*

1820

James Monroe	Democratic-Republican	231
John Quincy Adams	Independent-Republican	1
Votes not cast		*3*

1824

John Quincy Adams	Democratic-Republican	84
Andrew Jackson	Democratic-Republican	99
William H. Crawford	Democratic-Republican	41
Henry Clay	Democratic-Republican	37

1828

Andrew Jackson	Democratic	178
John Quincy Adams	National Republican	83

1832		
Andrew Jackson	Democratic	219
Henry Clay	National Republican	49
John Floyd	Independent	11
William Wirt	Anti-Masonic	7
Votes not cast		2

1836		
Martin Van Buren	Democratic	170
William H. Harrison	Whig	73
Hugh L. White	Whig	26
Daniel Webster	Whig	14
W. P. Magnum	Whig	11

1840		
William H. Harrison	Whig	234
Martin Van Buren	Democratic	60

1844		
James K. Polk	Democratic	170
Henry Clay	Whig	105
James G. Birney	Liberty	0
Martin Van Buren	Free-Soil	0

1848		
Zachary Taylor	Whig	163
Lewis Cass	Democratic	127
Martin Van Buren	Free-Soil	0

1852		
Franklin Pierce	Democratic	254
Winfield Scott	Whig	42
John P. Hale	Free-Soil	0

1856		
James Buchanan	Democratic	174
John C. Frémont	Republican	114
Millard Fillmore	American	8

1860			
Abraham Lincoln	Republican	180	
John C. Breckinridge	Democratic	72	
John Bell	Constitutional Union	39	
Stephen A. Douglas	Democratic	12	

1864			
Abraham Lincoln	Republican	212	
George B. McClellan	Democratic	21	

1868			
Ulysses S. Grant	Republican	214	
Horatio Seymour	Democratic	80	
Votes not counted		*23*	

1872			
Ulysses S. Grant	Republican	286	3,597,132
Horace Greeley	Dem.-Lib. Republican	66*	2,834,125
Thomas A. Hendricks	Democratic	42	
B. Gratz Brown	Dem.-Lib. Republican	18	
Charles J. Jenkins	Democratic	2	
David Davis	Independent	1	
Votes not counted		*17*	

**When Horace Greeley (1811-1872) died before the electoral college met in 1872, his votes were divided among the other candidates.*

1876			
Rutherford B. Hayes	Republican	185	4,033,768
Samuel J. Tilden	Democratic	184	4,285,992
Peter Cooper	Greenback	0	81, 737
1880			
James A. Garfield	Republican	214	4,449,053
Winfield Hancock	Democratic	155	4,442,035
James B. Weaver	Greenback	0	308,578
1884			
Grover Cleveland	Democratic	219	4,911,017
James G. Blaine	Republican	182	4,848,334
Benjamin Butler	Greenback	0	175,370
John St. John	Prohibition	0	150,369
1888			
Benjamin Harrison	Republican	233	5,440,216
Grover Cleveland	Democratic	168	5,538,233
Clinton Fisk	Prohibition	0	249,506
Alson Streeter	Union Labor	0	146,935
1892			
Grover Cleveland	Democratic	277	5,556,918
Benjamin Harrison	Republican	145	5,176,108
James B. Weaver	People's	22	1,041,028
John Bidwell	Prohibition	0	264,133
1896			
William McKinley	Republican	271	7,035,638
William Jennings Bryan	Democratic-People's	176	6,467,946
John Palmer	National Democratic	0	133,148
Joshua Levering	Prohibition	0	132,007
1900			
William McKinley	Republican	292	7,219,530
William Jennings Bryan	Democratic-People's	155	6,358,071
John G. Woolley	Prohibition	0	208,914
Eugene V. Debs	**Social Democratic**	**0**	**94,768**

1904			
Theodore Roosevelt	Republican	336	7,628,834
Alton B. Parker	Democratic	140	5,084,491
Eugene V. Debs	**Socialist**	**0**	**402,400**
1908			
William Howard Taft	Republican	321	7,679,006
William Jennings Bryan	Democratic	162	6,409,106
Eugene V. Debs	**Socialist**	**0**	**402,820**
1912			
Woodrow Wilson	Democratic	435	6,286,214
Theodore Roosevelt	**Progressive**	**88**	**4,126,020**
William Howard Taft	Republican	8	3,483,922
Eugene V. Debs	**Socialist**	**0**	**897,011**
1916			
Woodrow Wilson	Democratic	277	9,129,606
Charles E. Hughes	Republican	254	8,538,221
A. L. Benson	Socialist	0	585,113
1920			
Warren Harding	Republican	404	16,152,200
James M. Cox	Democratic	127	9,147,353
Eugene V. Debs	**Socialist**	**0**	**917,799**
1924			
Calvin Coolidge	Republican	382	15,725,016
John W. Davis	Democratic	136	8,385,586
Robert M. La Follette	**Progressive**	**13**	**4,822,856**
1928			
Herbert Hoover	Republican	444	21,392,190
Alfred E. Smith	Democratic	87	15,016,443
Norman Thomas	Socialist	0	267,420

1932			
Franklin D. Roosevelt	Democratic	472	22,821,857
Herbert Hoover	Republican	59	15,761,841
Norman Thomas	Socialist	0	884,781
1936			
Franklin D. Roosevelt	Democratic	523	27,751,597
Alfred M. Landon	Republican	8	16,679,583
Norman Thomas	Socialist	0	187,720
1940			
Franklin D. Roosevelt	Democratic	449	27,244,160
Wendell L. Wilkie	Republican	82	22,305,198
Norman Thomas	Socialist	0	99,557
1944			
Franklin D. Roosevelt	Democratic	432	25,602,504
Thomas E. Dewey	Republican	99	22,006,285
Norman Thomas	Socialist	0	80,518
1948			
Harry S Truman	Democratic	303	24,179,345
Thomas E. Dewey	Republican	189	21,991,291
Strom Thurmond	**States' Rights**	**39**	**1,176,125**
Henry A. Wallace	**Progressive**	**0**	**1,157,326**
Norman Thomas	Socialist	0	139,572
1952			
Dwight D. Eisenhower	Republican	442	33,936,234
Adlai E. Stevenson	Democratic	89	27,314,992
1956			
Dwight D. Eisenhower	Republican	457	35,590,472
Adlai E. Stevenson	Democratic	73	26,022,752
1960			
John F. Kennedy	Democratic	303	34,226,731
Richard M. Nixon	Republican	219	34,108,157
Harry F. Byrd	Independent	15	482,067

1964			
Lyndon B. Johnson	Democratic	486	43,129,484
Barry M. Goldwater	Republican	52	27,178,188

1968			
Richard M. Nixon	Republican	301	31,785,480
Hubert H. Humphrey	Democratic	191	31,275,166
George C. Wallace	**American Independent**	**46**	**9,906,473**

1972			
Richard M. Nixon	Republican	520	47,169,911
George S. McGovern	Democratic	17	29,170,383
John Schmitz	American	0	1,099,482

1976			
Jimmy Carter	Democratic	297	40,830,763
Gerald R. Ford	Republican	240	39,147,973
Eugene McCarthy	Independent	0	756,631

1980			
Ronald Reagan	Republican	489	43,899,248
Jimmy Carter	Democratic	49	36,481,435
John B. Anderson	**Independent**	**0**	**5,719,437**

1984			
Ronald Reagan	Republican	525	54,455,075
Walter F. Mondale	Democratic	13	37,577,185

1988			
George Bush	Republican	426	48,886,097
Michael Dukakis	Democratic	111	41,809,074

1992			
Bill Clinton	Democratic	370	44,909,889
George Bush	Republican	168	39,104,545
Ross Perot	**Independent**	**0**	**19,742,267**

Bibliography

"Anderson, John B(ayard)." *Current Biography.* New York: H. W. Wilson Co., 1979.

Blum, John Morton, ed. *The Price of Vision: The Diary of Henry A. Wallace.* Boston: Houghton Mifflin, 1973.

"Campaign '80: The Third Man." *Newsweek*, May 5, 1980.

Digregorio, William A. *The Complete Book of the U.S. Presidents.* New York: Barricade Books, 1993.

"Dixiecrat Medley." *Time*, October 4, 1948.

Erico, Charles, and J. Samuel Walker. "The New Deal and the Guru." *American Heritage*, March 1989.

Frady, Marshall. *Wallace.* New York: World, 1968.

Kruschke, Earl R. *Encyclopedia of Third Party Candidates in the United States.* Santa Barbara: ABC-CLIO, 1991.

Miller, Nathan. *Theodore Roosevelt: A Life.* New York: Morrow, 1992.

Morganthau, Tom. "Citizen Perot." *Newsweek*, November 9, 1992.

Morganthau, Tom, and Ron LaBecque. "Politics of Principle, The." *Newsweek*, March 3, 1980.

"New South: A Political Phenomenon Grips Dixie's Voters." *Newsweek*, October 25, 1948.

"Perot, H. Ross." *Current Biography*. New York: H. W. Wilson, 1971.

Phillips, C. "That Baffling Personality, Mr. Wallace," *New York Times Magazine*, February 8, 1948.

Seal, Mark. "Retro Man," *Esquire*, July 1992.

Thelen, David P. *Robert M. La Follette and the Insurgent Spirit*. Madison: University of Wisconsin Press, 1985.

"Thurmond, Strom." *Current Biography*. New York: H. W. Wilson Co., 1948.

"Wallace's Last Message." *National Review*, May 9, 1968.

Whitman, Alden, ed. *American Reformers*. New York: H. W. Wilson, 1985.

Wright, Lawrence. *If Elected . . . Unsuccessful Candidates for the Presidency, 1796-1968*. Washington, DC: Smithsonian Institution, 1972.

Index

ABOUT THE AUTHOR

NATHAN AASENG is a widely published writer of books for young adults. He has covered a diverse range of subjects, including history, biography, social issues, sports, business, science, and fiction. Aaseng is also the author of *Great Justices of the Supreme Court*, *You Are the Supreme Court Justice*, *You Are the President*, *You Are the President II: 1800-1899*, *You Are the General*, and the forthcoming book, *You Are the General II: 1800-1899.* He lives in Eau Claire, Wisconsin, with his wife and children.

Photo Credits

Photographs courtesy of the Bettmann Archive: pp. 6, 84, 92, 98, 107 (top), 116, 123, 128, 137, 141, 142; Library of Congress, pp. 11 (both), 14, 18, 20, 25, 26 (both), 29, 32, 35, 36, 38, 43, 45, 47, 52, 57, 63, 65, 72, 78, 95, 100, 109, 111, 113 (right), 124, 127, 138, 143; Cornell University, pp. 33, 66, 81, 93; Eugene V. Debs Foundation, Terre Haute, Indiana, pp. 48, 50; Idaho State Historical Society, p. 80; State Historical Society of Iowa, Iowa City, pp. 68, 75, 82; South Caroliniana Library, p. 86; South Carolina Historical Society, pp. 88, 91; Strom Thurmond, p. 99; Lyndon Baines Johnson Library, p. 107 (bottom); State of Alabama Department of History and Archives, p. 108; Minnesota Historical Society, pp. 113 (left), 148; State Historical Society of Wisconsin, p. 126; United We Stand America, Inc., p. 130; and the White House, p. 144.